- Clapton's **LAYLA** will drive you to your knees . . .
- She might not be Michael's, but **BILLIE JEAN** could be yours . . .
- The Dead said to call him **CASEY**, 'cause *he's* driving that train . . .
- The Everly Brothers' **SUZIE** would rather snooze than cruise . . .
- Mr. Taylor tells you who's a sweet baby: **JAMES** . . .
- Richard may be little, but his **SALLY** is long and tall . . .
- What will everyone say to **RHONDA**? *Help me!*

ROCK 'N' ROLL BABY NAMES

ROCK 'N' ROLL
BABY NAMES

ERIC THOROMAN

AVON BOOKS ◆ NEW YORK

AVON BOOKS, INC.
1350 Avenue of the Americas
New York, New York 10019

Copyright © 1998 by Eric Thoroman
Published by arrangement with the author
Visit our website at **http://www.AvonBooks.com**
Library of Congress Catalog Card Number: 98-93122
ISBN: 0-380-79721-6

First Avon Books Printing: November 1998

AVON TRADEMARK REG. U.S. PAT. OFF. AND IN OTHER COUNTRIES, MARCA
REGISTRADA, HECHO EN U.S.A.

Printed in the U.S.A.

WCD   10 9 8 7 6 5 4 3 2 1

For Ann McKay

She's my heart's delight

Preface

You're having a baby—congratulations!

Joyful as this time is, preparing for the baby is also a nerve-wracking experience—and not just struggling through Lamaze classes, decorating the baby's room, and making day-care arrangements. No, these responsibilities pale when compared to the task that makes many soon-to-be parents sweat and shudder: *naming* that little bundle of joy.

The pressure can be enormous. Your Uncle Bert will remind you that every male in your family has had the name Albert for the last two hundred years. Meanwhile, your mother will be swift to hint that she'll be hurt if a daughter isn't named after her: Gladys. And just when you think you've found the perfect name—Eileen, let's say—you realize Eileen was your grandmother's name. No problem, you say—just use the other grandmother's name for a middle name? Well, what if the other grandmother's name was Gertrude—and you *hate* the name Gertrude? (Sorry, all you Gertrudes.)

That's where *Rock 'n' Roll Baby Names* comes in. It's simply a matter of getting your priorities straight. So, rather than trying to please every relative who's living (or ever lived), you can go to a higher authority: rock 'n' roll music.

Just think—rather than fawning to Uncle Morty or Grandma Bertha, you can name your baby after your favorite rock song or group. So say goodbye to names you don't like and offending relatives you never knew; say hello to fun names like Johnny (*B. Goode*) and Sara (*Smile*).

How do you find a rock 'n' roll baby name? It's easy. You have two ways to choose. If you have a name or song in mind,

1

look through the ''By Name'' section, and see what songs are available. Or, if you'd rather immortalize a group or artist, check the ''By Group'' section.

Either way, happy name hunting!

Part 1
BY NAME

Most people have a song that tends to follow them around. If your name is Veronica, people will forever be warbling the Elvis Costello refrain to you; ditto if you go by *Roxanne* or *Billie Jean*. Songs will tell you to "be good" (Johnny), to "smile" (Sara, Rosemary), to be "careful with that axe" (Eugene). Songs describe your size (*Big Bad John*), your demeanor (*Big Bad John*), your sex appeal (*Sexy Sadie*).

Your baby will be no different. But with *Rock 'n' Roll Baby Names*, you can take the matter into your own hands and choose how your child will be immortalized. In this section, you can browse more than four hundred names and see what rock 'n' roll songs feature these names. Some will be famous, some obscure; some will be cute, some mean and nasty. But whatever you're looking for, you'll find the perfect rockin' baby name waiting for you!

Abigail
Abigail Beecher   Freddy "Boom Boom" Cannon

Abraham
Abraham, Martin, and John   Dion

If you've given birth to a little Abe Lincoln (you know, top hat, beard, six-foot-four), consider this atypical number by Dion from the late sixties, when earnest political anthems were in fashion. The names in the song refer to various martyred political heroes. Not that you want a martyr, but what's wrong with naming a child after Honest Abe?

ANOTHER ROCKIN' ABRAHAM SONG

Bosom of Abraham   Elvis Presley

Adam
Adam's Apple   Aerosmith
Adam Raised a Cain   Bruce Springsteen

These Adam songs really rock—*hard*. If it's a hard-rockin' Adam you have on your hands, you can raise rockin' Cain with either of these songs.

You may want your child to wear earplugs if he's going to be exposed to this kind of rock. Then again, babies seem

5

to have their own amps cranked up all the way—have you heard one wail lately?

OTHER ROCKIN' ADAM SONGS

Adam and Evil   Elvis Presley
Adam in Chains   Billy Idol

Adelaide
Adelaide   John Cale

Adrian
Adrian   Eurythmics

Agnes
St. Agnes and the Burning Train   Sting

Aja
Aja   Steely Dan

Al
You Can Call Me Al   Paul Simon

Some children are born forty—"soft in the middle, with a life that's so hard," as the song goes. Come to think of it, *all* babies are soft in the middle, and from their perspective, life probably *is* hard. How would you like it if you couldn't hold your own head up?

But don't cry for your baby, just name him Al, and promise to be his "bodyguard and long-lost pal."

Aladdin
Aladdin Sane   David Bowie

Alan
Alan's Psychedelic Breakfast   Pink Floyd
Alan Watts Blues   Van Morrison

Albert

Uncle Albert/Admiral Halsey   Paul and Linda
McCartney

Sometimes your little boy will have to face grave disappointments. You know, stuff that shakes the earth: Johnny got better Christmas gifts. Someone forgot to tape his favorite program. There are no french fries on this menu!

For these times and many others, the McCartney song will fit the bill. You can sing to your little Albert about how *sorry* you are.

ANOTHER ROCKIN' ALBERT SONG

Frankie and Albert   Bob Dylan

Alberta

Alberta #1   Bob Dylan
Alberta #2   Bob Dylan
Alberta   John Lee Hooker

Alexander

Alexander the Medium   Jefferson Airplane

Ali

Ali Click   Brian Eno

Alice

White Rabbit   Jefferson Airplane

This song blew the mind of AM radio back in the sixties. And it was hard to censor it—after all, it was merely a recanting of the beloved children's classic *Alice's Adventures in Wonderland*. Unfortunately, what nobody had noticed for decades was that the author, Lewis Carroll, was *on drugs*.

That's not to say this isn't a good song for an adventurous and imaginative little Alice. The enchantment of the story still manages to come through—but if you sing or play this song for your little girl, you may want to amend the lyrics a bit. The dope-pipe reference should be cut, and the famous last line, about nourishing one's cranium, can be changed to something innocuous and practical, say: "eat your beans" or "clean your room." Use your imagination.

OTHER ROCKIN' ALICE SONGS

Alice's Restaurant Arlo Guthrie
Alice Ling Tommy Boyce and Bobby Hart

Alison
Alison Elvis Costello

If you enjoy hunting, pitching baseballs, skeet shooting, or (God forbid) shooting apples off of people's heads, you may want to name your girl Alison, after this Elvis Costello hit. After all, you're going to need to assure her constantly that your "aim is true."

ANOTHER ROCKIN' ALISON SONG

Memories of Allison Spinners

Althea
Althea Grateful Dead

Amanda
Amanda Boston
Miss Amanda Jones Rolling Stones

Amelia
Amelia   Joni Mitchell

Amy
Amie   Pure Prairie League

This mellow little country-reel song, a somewhat watered-down country-bluegrass concoction, was a big hit in the seventies and popularized the less-common spelling of Amy. Simple and catchy, easy to play and sing, it found its way into about every coffeehouse and live-music saloon in the land.

It's a pretty sweet baby song, too. If you think you'll stay with your little Amie for a while, maybe longer (and one would hope you would), *Amie*'s a good one for you. Your little girl will feel secure and loved—even if she tires of the twangy vocals.

ANOTHER ROCKIN' AMY SONG

Amy   Elton John

Amos
Amos Moses   Jerry Reed

Andrew
Man on the Moon   R. E. M.

You may have the mixed blessing of having a child who reminds you of Andy Kaufman, the cracked comedian best remembered as Latka on the sitcom "Taxi." Perhaps your child likes to do Elvis impersonations, speaks in a fey foreign accent, loves wrestling, enjoys lip-synching to Mighty Mouse recordings?

All right, it's unlikely, but just in case you do, this R.E.M. song—a tribute to the wacky comic—is for you.

Angel

Angel of the Morning   Marilee Rush

With this name, you can sing Angel songs and never repeat yourself—below is actually a fairly *small* sample of the songs available.

The Marilee Rush number is among the most famous. Useful, too: "They call you angel of the morning!" you can bellow at your baby as you're providing the 2 a.m. bottle for the umpteenth straight week. This tune might help you keep your spirits up when you're getting less sleep than a night watchman.

Angel of Harlem   U2
Angel Baby (Don't You Ever   Stevie Wonder
Leave)
Angel From Montgomery   John Prine, Carly
                          Simon, Bonnie Raitt
Thank You For Sending Me   Talking Heads
An Angel
Angel Eyes   Roxy Music
Angel of Mercy   Dire Straits
When the Angels Fall   Sting
Angel   Bonnie Raitt
Contacting My Angel   Van Morrison
Across the Bridge Where   Van Morrison
Angels Dwell
Blue Angel   Roy Orbison
Angel   Poco
Cowboys and Angels   George Michael
Tin Angel   Joni Mitchell
I'm Your Angel   John Lennon
Angel Dance   Los Lobos
Angels With Dirty Faces   Los Lobos
Angel (What in the World's   Atlanta Rhythm Section
Come Over Us)
Angels Don't Fall in Love   Bangles
Angel   Eurythmics
Angel   Rod Stewart
Our Little Angel   Elvis Costello
Fallen Angel   Bee Gees
Fallen Angel   Blue Oyster Cult
Angel   Neil Diamond
Angel   Jimi Hendrix
Angel Flying Too Close to   Willie Nelson
the Ground
City of Angels   Journey

Angela

Angela   Mötley Crüe
Angela   Toto
Free Angela   Santana
Angela   John Lennon

Angelica
Angelica   Richard Marx

Angelina
Farewell, Angelina   Bob Dylan

Angeline
Angeline   Elton John

Angelique
Angelique   Kenny Loggins

Angie
Angie   Rolling Stones
Angie Baby   Helen Reddy

The Helen Reddy number is certainly a one-song-fits-all-babies song. If Helen Reddy is your thing, go for it.

Then again, you may have more of a Rolling Stones kind of baby (which could be scary). And while *Angie* may not seem the most obvious source for a baby name, this song could be useful. Someday your Angie may be a teenager full of attitude—self-conscious, hypercritical, and quick to point out her parents' faults. "Angie," you can then wail to her, "you can't say we never tried."

OTHER ROCKIN' ANGIE SONGS

Angie Girl   Stevie Wonder
Anji   Simon and Garfunkel

Ann
The Weight   The Band
Annie's Song   John Denver

Two very different songs here—and both fitting for naming your baby.

The Band song is useful if you're feeling the pressure—the weight—of parenthood. You can wail the refrain of this song whenever it's getting to you that you've just added a dependent to your life for the next the next, oh, thirty years. So wail away (and save for college).

The sweet John Denver song is for a little Annie of your senses. And parenthood *is* a sensuous experience—as any parent who's sensed baby breath, dirty diapers, and wet baby burps knows.

OTHER ROCKIN' ANN SONGS

Work With Me, Annie   Hank Ballard
Annie Had a Baby   Hank Ballard
Annie's Other Song   John Denver
Polk Salad Annie   Tony Joe White
Annie Get Your Gun   Squeeze
Annie Christian   Prince
Sidewalk Annie   Wallflowers
Miss Ann   Little Richard
Annie is Back   Little Richard
Annie Mae   John Lee Hooker

Anna
Anna (Go to Him)   Beatles
Anna Lee, the Healer   Beach Boys
Anna   Toto
Anna Stasia   Prince

Annabella
Wicked Annabella   Kinks

Anthony
Anthony Boy   Chuck Berry

April
April Come She Will   Simon and Garfunkel
Pieces of April   Three Dog Night

Arizona
Arizona   Mark Lindsay

Not the most common baby name in the world. But if you identify with the Nicholas Cage and Holly Hunter characters in the film *Raising Arizona*, this a good one for you. (Just don't kidnap anyone, okay?)

Arnold
Arnold Layne   Joe Boyd

Arthur
MacArthur Park   Donna Summer (originally Richard Harris)

This number, penned by the sixties songwriting phenom Jimmy Webb, frequently makes critics' lists of all-time worst songs, mainly because of the combination of the dramatic melody, overproduction, and inexplicably turgid lyrics. It's all the more notorious for being a major *Billboard* hit *twice*—last by disco queen Donna Summer.

Not that it's a bad baby name song. You can always make up your *own* bad lyrics—especially as a way of fostering good behavior as little Arthur gets older. For instance, you can sing: "Someone left his toys out in the yard!" "Someone left his french fries in the bath!" "Someone left his undies on the floor!" The possibilities are endless, especially if your Arthur is like most kids, and inclined to leave his things everywhere but where they're *supposed* to be.

OTHER ROCKIN' ARTHUR SONGS

Arthur's Theme   Christopher Cross
Arthur McBride   Bob Dylan
Uncle Arthur   David Bowie
Port Arthur High School   Janis Joplin
Arthur   Kinks

Athena
Athena   Who

Barbara

Barbara Ann   Beach Boys (originally Regents)

A wonderful sing-along song that can be appreciated by the youngest of kids. (Don't be offended if your child sings the opening syllables of this song even before she says "Mama" and "Dada.")

So, if you've considered such names as Peggy Sue, and pondered the merits of Betty Lou, but knew they just weren't adequate, go for Barbara Ann.

This could work, too, if you're helping your child count sheep: "Baa baa baa baa Baabara Ann!"

ANOTHER ROCKIN' BARBARA SONG

Major Barbara   Aerosmith

Barry

Barrytown   Steely Dan
Berry Rides Again   Steppenwolf

Belinda

Belinda   Roy Orbison
Belinda   Eurythmics

Benjamin
Bennie and the Jets   Elton John

A fitting tune if your son is destined to join the Air Force, or NASA, or even—a stretch—the New Jersey football team.

Be careful, though. This is one of those *dangerous* songs, if you're a dad and you're actually thinking about singing this song to your little boy. Dads attempting to sing in this range sometimes hurt themselves—and even young babies will give them that "You're *weird*" look.

OTHER ROCKIN' BENJAMIN SONGS

Ben   Michael Jackson
Benny the Bouncer   Emerson, Lake, and Palmer

Bernadette
Bernadette   Four Tops

Bernard
Uncle Bernie's Farm   Zappa/Mothers
Bernard Jenkins   Eric Clapton

Bertha
Bertha   Grateful Dead
Bertha   Los Lobos

Bess/Beth/Betty (*see* Elizabeth)

Beulah
Beulah   Devo

Bill, Billy (*see* William)

Billie Jean
Billie Jean   Michael Jackson

Well, if you want to name your daughter Billie Jean, and

you're a big fan of Michael Jackson, she will inevitably be associated with this song. Given that this is more of a rockin' that's-*not*-my-baby song, this could change your mind about naming your girl Billie Jean!

If she grows up to be like the Billie Jean in this song, she might find herself in a paternity suit with Mr. Jackson himself. Wouldn't *that* be a thriller!

Billie Joe
Ode To Billie Joe   Bobbie Gentry

Bo
Bo Diddley   Bob Seger
Bo's Guitar   Bo Diddley
Bo's Bounce   Bo Diddley
Bo Diddley   Buddy Holly

Bobby (female)
Bobby Jean   Bruce Springsteen

Bob/Bobby (male; *see* Robert)

Bonnie
Bonnie   Supertramp
Bonny   AC/DC

Bonzo
Bonzo's Montreux   Led Zeppelin

Boris
Boris, the Spider   Who

Brandy
Brandy (You're a Fine Girl)   Looking Glass

"It's a fine girl," your doctor might exclaim when you have your little girl. So, you've got a fine girl—what do you call her? Well, there's always Brandy.

Don't take too many of the song's lyrics to heart, though—unless you're expecting your Brandy's heart to be perpetually broken by wayward sailors.

Brenda
Brenda X   Poco

Buddy
Buddy's Song   Fleetwood Mac
Buddy   Willie Nelson

Caesar
Little Caesar   Kiss
Caesar   Iggy Pop

Cain
Adam Raised a Cain   Bruce Springsteen
Blame It on Cain   Elvis Costello

Candida
Candida   Dawn

Candy
Candy's Room   Bruce Springsteen
Candy Girl   Four Seasons
Candy Everybody Wants   10,000 Maniacs
Candy Man   Roy Orbison (originally Fred Neil)
Candy-O   Cars

Carmelita
Carmelita   Linda Ronstadt

Carmen
Carmen   Toto
Soul of Carmen Miranda   John Cale

Carol
Oh! Carol   Neil Sedaka
Carol   Rolling Stones
Carol   Chuck Berry
Carol of the Bells   Four Seasons

Caroline
Sweet Caroline   Neil Diamond

The emphasis here is on *sweet*. This one isn't for everyone (for many it's *too* sweet), but it could work for you. Neil Diamond's foot-tapper, a monster hit when it first came out, expresses completely warm and uncomplicated sentiments for his Caroline.

If you've got a little sunshiny Caroline and a musical sweet tooth, go for it. Having a baby never felt so good.

OTHER ROCKIN' CAROLINE SONGS

Caroline No   Brian Wilson
Caroline   Jefferson Starship
Caroline   Fleetwood Mac
Caroline (Are You Ready For   Steppenwolf
the Outlaw World)
Carolina On My Mind   James Taylor
Caroline Says (I and II)   Lou Reed
Woman Going Crazy on   Jimmy Buffett
Caroline Street

Carrie
Carrie   Europe
Carey   Joni Mitchell

Carrie-Ann
Carrie-Ann   Hollies

This charming song, belted out by Graham Nash (later of Crosby, Stills, and Nash), could be your all-purpose number as your little girl starts to play games—both formal games (like board games) and the usual kidding around. "Hey, Carrie-Ann," you can ask her, "can anybody play?"

Casey
Casey Jones   Grateful Dead

This classic anthem, the saga of various railroad employees who have very low safety standards, is enough to make one prefer skydiving as a relatively sanguine mode of transportation.

It's hard to picture it as a song you'd share with your little one. Audible cocaine snorts, blatant drug references, and the aforementioned rather lax attitude about rail safety . . . all make *Casey* one of those songs that gives Tipper Gore a reason to be.

Not that Casey's a bad name. But you may not want to tell your Casey what inspired his name until he's about, oh, thirty.

ANOTHER ROCKIN' CASEY SONG

Casey at the Bat   John Cale

Cassidy
Cassidy   Grateful Dead

Cathy (*see also* Kathleen)
Cathy's Clown   Everly Brothers

Cecilia
Cecilia   Simon and Garfunkel

Babies can have you around their little fingers sometimes—"breaking your heart, shaking your confidence." This sometimes gets worse as they grow up. Your little girl may stay out late, and you may find yourself on your knees, begging her "please to come home."

If this sounds like your little girl, you may have a Cecilia on your hands.

Charles
Charlie Brown   Coasters

21

The Coasters classic will fit your boy if he's a little cutup, a lovable clown, and has a bit of bad luck—the kind who always manages to take the rap whether he's guilty or innocent.

Of course, in this day and age the chances of your child calling an English teacher "Daddy-O" are remote. But you never know.

OTHER ROCKIN' CHARLES SONGS

Chuck E.'s in Love   Rickie Lee Jones
Goodtime Charlie's Got the   Danny O'Keefe
Blues
Charlie Freak   Steely Dan
Cosmic Charlie   Grateful Dead
Mr. Charlie   Grateful Dead
St. Charles   Jefferson Starship

Charlotte
Charlotte Sometimes   Cure

Charro
Charro!   Elvis Presley

Chelsea
Chelsea Morning   Joni Mitchell

Bill and Hillary (yes, *that* Bill and Hillary) named their only child after this Joni Mitchell song. So why not name your baby the same? Who knows, she might grow up to be president someday—or at least a president's daughter.

Cherry
Cherry, Cherry   Neil Diamond

Chico
Papa Come Quick (Jody and Chico)   Bonnie Raitt

Chiquita
Chiquita   Aerosmith

Chloe
Chloe   Elton John

Christopher
Christopher Tracy's Song   Prince
Hang On St. Christopher   Rod Stewart

Christie
Christie Lee   Billy Joel

Christine
Christine Sixteen   Kiss

You may think when your girl is in her mid-teens (which will happen in a blink) that she'll be as sweet as LeAnn Rimes and that you can throw her a sweet sixteen party. Well, more likely she'll have an *attitude* and will be surrounded by slimy guys. And the only thing she'll find interesting about her parents are your old Kiss records.

In which case, she may not be a sweet sixteen but more of a *Christine Sixteen*—after the Kiss rocker about the girl who's too young but still drives men crazy.

Chuck (see Charles)

Cindy
Cindy's Birthday   Johnny Crawford
Cindy C.   Prince
Cindy Tells Me   Brian Eno
Cindy's Lament   Rod Stewart

Cissy
Cissy Strut   The Meters

Claire
Planet Claire   B-52s

Sometimes your daughter may seem otherworldly, the "baby from another planet." And if you like the cheeky and spacy B-52s sounds, *Planet Claire* may be the anthem for your little extraterrestrial.

You can answer your girl's "Where did I come from?" questions with this song: "You came from the Planet Claire." It's certainly no more outrageous than saying the stork brought her.

ANOTHER ROCKIN' CLAIRE SONG

Clair   Gilbert O'Sullivan

Clancy
Nowadays Clancy Can't Even Sing   Buffalo Springfield

Claudette
Claudette   Roy Orbison

Yes, your daughter is pretty. Of course. Yes, she's the prettiest. Oh yes, definitely. And of course, everybody *says* that about their daughter, but let's face it, in your case it's *true*.

So consider *Claudette*. For your "pretty little girl"—

Claudette. With this Roy Orbison tune, you can sing her pretty praises forever.

ANOTHER ROCKIN' CLAUDETTE SONG

Lawdy Miss Clawdy   Lloyd Price

Cody
Cody's Song   Kenny Loggins

Connie
Connie-O   Four Seasons

Corinna
Corinna, Corinna   Ray Peterson

You may be one who likes to say a name over and over again. If so, you may want a song with a refrain that has nothing *but* the name.

Corinna, Corinna could work. Sing this song to your child from the time she's an infant, and she'll know her name before she can say "goo."

Crystal
Crystal   Fleetwood Mac

Curtis
Ballad of Curtis Lowe   Lynyrd Skynyrd

Daisy
Dazie Mae   John Lee Hooker

Daniel
Danny Boy   Conway Twitty, Carly Simon, Labelle

It's not rock 'n' roll, but this traditional Irish folk song has been covered by so many rockers (and even those as far afield as Labelle) that it might as well be.

So if you want to honor your Irish heritage but still want a little rockin' in your baby's name, Danny's the one.

OTHER ROCKIN' DANIEL SONGS

Danny's Song   Anne Murray, Loggins and Messina
Daniel   Elton John
Dan Dare (Pilot of the Future)   Elton John
The Ballad of Danny Bailey   Elton John
(1909-34)
Danny   Elvis Presley
Daniel and the Sacred Harp   The Band
Dan, My Fling   Carly Simon
Danny Says   Ramones
Danny's All-Star Joint   Rickie Lee Jones

Daphne
Daphne   Squeeze

Darcy
Darcy Farrow   John Denver

Darlene
Darlene   Led Zeppelin

Davanita
Davanita   Pearl Jam

David
Davy the Fat Boy   Randy Newman
Black Jack Davey   Bob Dylan
Dave's Gone Skiing   Toto
Little David   James Taylor
Davy   Carly Simon
David Watts   Kinks, Jam

Dawn
Dawn (Go Away)   Four Seasons
Delta Dawn   Helen Reddy

Dean
James Dean   Eagles

Deannie
Hey Deannie   Shaun Cassidy

His father was actor Jack Cassidy, his mother played Mom Partridge, and his half-brother was David Cassidy. And even someone born with all of these silver spoons can still have a hard time getting on the radio—but Shaun Cassidy did, in the seventies, with such numbers as *Hey Deannie*.

If bubblegum teen idols are your thing and if you like performers whose average audience age is about twelve, then Deannie may be the name for you.

Deborah
Debbie Denise   Blue Oyster Cult

Dee
Ellis Dee   Jimmy Buffett

Deirdre
Deirdre   Beach Boys

Delia
Delia   Bob Dylan (traditional)

Delilah
Samson and Delilah   Grateful Dead
Delilah   Tom Jones
Beautiful Delilah   Chuck Berry
Delilah   Queen

Denise
Denise   Randy and the Rainbows

Oh, for a love so unbridled, so true . . . But wait a minute, that's exactly the way you feel about your little girl. If she's a little blue-eyed love, *Denise* is perfect.

And someday, when she's older, pesky boys chasing her will serenade her with this song and make complete idiots of themselves.

ANOTHER ROCKIN' DENISE SONG

Debbie Denise   Blue Oyster Cult

Dennis
The Ballad (Denny and Jean)   Todd Rundgren
Denis   Blondie

Desiree
Desiree   Neil Diamond
Desiree   Left Banke
Deseri   Zappa/Mothers

Diana

Diana   Paul Anka

In this classic fifties anthem, the singer beseeches his Diana to please stay with him. You may think that's not a fitting theme for your new baby, who, so long as she's immobile, isn't going anywhere. But then again, in a blink she going to be walking, and then suddenly you'll have the need to get her to stay with you. By the time she's a terrible two, you'll be pulling out all of the stops. *Diana* will fit this bill.

   Trivia: Diminutive Paul Anka was just fifteen when he wrote and recorded this anthem—his first big hit. The precocious lounge lizard also dated mousketeers, and had songs written *about* him (*see* Paul).

ANOTHER ROCKIN' DIANA SONG

Dirty Diana   Michael Jackson

Diane

Jack and Diane   John Cougar Mellencamp
Little Diane   Dion
My Diane   Beach Boys
Oh Diane   Fleetwood Mac

Dixie

The Night They Drove Old Dixie Down   The Band

Maybe not a perfect baby name song as it is, but modify the lyrics just slightly and you've got a good lullaby: *The Night They Put Old Dixie Down* can be a companion to a bedtime story (say, *Goodnight Moon*) as you cajole your daughter to sleep every night.

Dolly
Hello, Dolly   Louis Armstrong

It's a stretch to include this in the rock category. Nonetheless, this single was a big hit in the same year the Beatles invaded America, giving the great Satchmo AM airplay and exposing a broad audience to his inimitable singing and trumpet playing.

It's also a great baby song. Not only for its catchy, quasi-Dixie beat (great for teaching your little girl a few steps), but for the appealing hi-there sentiments. And in situations when you restore your child to her proper place—put her back in a high chair, remove her from the laundry room, get her off of a mantel—you can always croon to her that it's nice to see her back where she belongs.

Dominique
Dominique   Singing Nun

Don
Don Juan   Pet Shop Boys
Don Juan's Reckless Daughter   Joni Mitchell
Modern Don Juan   Buddy Holly

Donna
Oh Donna   Richie Valens

During rock 'n' roll's "golden age" there was hardly a prettier song than this gorgeous and tender ballad—one of just two hits (with *La Bamba*) from the short career of rock's first Hispanic star.

For a Donna who's tender and true and soft and sensitive, you can't go wrong.

OTHER ROCKIN' DONNA SONGS

Donna   10cc
Donna the Prima Donna   Dion
Donna Means Heartache   Gene Pitney
Prima Donna   Chicago

Dorita
Dorita—the Spirit   Lou Reed

Dorothy/Dottie
Dottie I Like It   Tommy Roe

Duncan
Duncan   Paul Simon

Dutch
Woody and Dutch on the Slow Train   Rickie Lee Jones

Dwight
Ballad of Dwight Fry   Alice Cooper

Earl
Earl Gray Fleetwood Mac

Edith
Edith and the Kingpin Joni Mitchell

Edmund
Wreck of the Edmund Fitzgerald Gordon Lightfoot

Edward/Eddie
Eddie, Are You Kidding? Zappa/Mothers
Eddie My Love The Teen Queens

Eileen
Come On Eileen Dexy's Midnight Runners

Eleanor
Elenore Turtles

Tricia Nixon's favorite rock group, the Turtles (who played the White House during her father's presidency), were waning in popularity when their label beckoned them for a hit; their response was *Elenore*, which was indeed a hit.

And it's also a great baby name song. Of course, that's assuming your child is *swell*, that she's your pride and joy, *et cetera*.

Eli
Eli's Coming   Three Dog Night (originally Laura Nyro)

Like most parents, you may think your baby boy is the cutest thing alive. And like some, you may think your child is *irresistible*, a little bundle of charisma who's going to break some hearts. And you may even think your child is—or is going to be—downright *studly*.

If so, consider *Eli's Coming*, a rousing rocker about an Eli who is so dangerous that his impending presence necessitates a warning, like when the Weather Bureau issues a Small Craft Alert.

Elisa
Elisa   Bee Gees

Elise
Letter to Elise   Cure

Elizabeth
Beth   Kiss

If you *must* name your child after a Kiss song (and heaven knows there are probably those of you out there who *must*), consider *Beth*.

Your daughter may later appreciate this choice—especially if she doesn't share your love of glam rock. After all, *Beth*, as Kiss's one and only ballad, lets you name your child after a Kiss song without any of that blinding glitter.

Eloise

Miss Eloise, Miss Eloise   John Lee Hooker

Elton

Elton's Song   Elton John

Elvis

Elvis Presley in America   U2
Calling Elvis   Dire Straits
Elvis Imitators   Jimmy Buffett

Emily

For Emily, Whenever I May   Simon and Garfunkel
Find Her

Goodness, you can't cram much more imagery into a song than is packed into this one. Organdy, crinoline, smoke, burgundy, juniper . . . why, you can practically *smell* this song. And it's so pretty—an ethereal reverie, soft and sensitive, a perfect vehicle for Art Garfunkel's soft, sensitive voice.

If you have an otherworldly girl, who's always in soft focus to you (and maybe smells like the perfume department), Emily may be the name.

Emma

Emma   Hot Chocolate
Big Leg Emma   Zappa/Mothers
Emma   Little River Band

Eric

The Eric Dolphy Memorial Barbeque   Zappa/Mothers

Esau

My Brother Esau   Grateful Dead

Esmerelda

Dearest Esmerelda   John Denver

You know, your baby name doesn't have to be some joke—
you can name your girl a sweet name that has a sweet song
to go with it. Why not *Dearest Esmerelda?* One in a long
line of pretty songs by John Denver, for a baby who is not
only dear, but the *dearest*.

Esther

Esther Be the One   ZZ Top

Ethel

Cold Ethyl   Alice Cooper

Eugene

Careful With That Axe, Eugene   Pink Floyd

Whether you've got a little girl with a gun (*see* Jane) or a son with a cleaver, the message is the same: dangerous weapons and tools should be kept out of the hands of children!

If you've got a little boy and you think this is going to be a problem, Eugene may be your name.

OTHER ROCKIN' EUGENE SONGS

Eugene's Lament   Elvis Presley
Papa Gene's Blues   The Monkees

Eunice
  Eunice Two-Step   Beausoleil

Evangeline
  Evangeline   The Band
  Evangelini   Los Lobos

Evelyn
  Evelyn, a Modified Dog   Zappa/Mothers

Faith

Faith   George Michael

If you've got a little mischievous girl who likes to play games, *Faith* may be your song and name. All the more so if your girl likes to—as the Sunshine Band's K. C. used to put it—"shake her booty." Because in the video for this song, you see more of George Michael's wiggling butt than anything else.

OTHER ROCKIN' FAITH SONGS

Faith Interlude   Santana
Faith in the Families   Poco
Interlude: Faith   Earth, Wind, and Fire
Leap of Faith   Kenny Loggins

Fanny

Fanny   Bee Gees
Short Fat Fannie   Larry Williams
Jiving Sister Fanny   Rolling Stones
Fanny Mae   Steve Miller

Fernando

Fernando   ABBA

ABBA lovers looking for any excuse to name a baby after this inimitable group will find the perfect name in Fernando. It's destiny—just "something in the air."

Floyd

Floyd the Barber   Nirvana
Pretty Boy Floyd   Byrds

Francine

Francine   ZZ Top

Frank

So Long, Frank Lloyd Wright   Simon and Garfunkel
Frank and Lola   Jimmy Buffett
Ballad of Sir Frankie Crisp   George Harrison

Frankie

Frankie's First Affair   Sade
Frankie and Albert   Bob Dylan
Frankie and Johnny   Elvis Presley

Franklin

Franklin's Tower   Grateful Dead

Fredrick

The Freddie   Freddie and the Dreamers

It doesn't get much more dorky than this. Some of you can probably remember a beyond-bizarre dance craze called "The Freddie" that lasted for a few minutes during the British Invasion of the sixties. This dance required lurching the torso forward while kicking up unbent legs—*Frankenstein a go go.*

Nonetheless, this may be just the distinction you want to give your child. And if he can master "The Freddie" at an early age, he may later have a career in horror movies.

OTHER ROCKIN' FRED SONGS

Fast Buck Freddie   Jefferson Starship
Hey Fredrick   Jefferson Airplane
Do The Freddie   The Original Cast

Gene (see Eugene)

Geoffrey (see also Jeff)
Sir Geoffrey Saved the World   Bee Gees

George (male)
Slow Down Georgie (She's Poison)   Elton John
St. George and the Dragon   Toto
King George Street   Squeeze
Bob George   Prince
Madame George   Van Morrison
Killing of Georgie   Rod Stewart

Georgette
Rene and Georgette Magritte   Paul Simon
with their Dog After the War

Georgia
Georgia On My Mind   Ray Charles

Not rock 'n' roll, really, but this rendition of the Hoagy Carmichael standard got enough airplay in the sixties to be a part of the rock era, and has become the signature version of the song.

It's fitting for a baby, too. Because your little Georgia is bound to be on your mind.

Georgie/Georgy (female)
Georgy Girl   Seekers

A song of the Austin Powers era, the kind of anthem that went with the mod brits of the mid-to-late sixties (even though the Seekers were American).

If your daughter looks like Twiggy, like she belongs in a large-checked miniskirt with knee-high go-go boots and ironed hair, she may well be a Georgy Girl.

Gina
Gina   Johnny Mathis

Ginger
Ginger Bread   Frankie Avalon

Gloria
Gloria   Shadows of Knight (originally Them)
Gloria   Laura Branigan

Two very different songs with the same title. Both were big hits in their respective eras.

The first is the stronger baby name song. Originally written and recorded by the teenaged Van Morrison for the group Them, it was the cover, by the one-hit group Shadows of the Knight, that got the airplay. As for your little girl—well, this song is *about* your baby. And it's a rare song indeed that teaches your baby how to spell her own name—what a bonus! *G - l - o - r - i - a!*

OTHER ROCKIN' GLORIA SONGS

Gloria's Eyes   Bruce Springsteen
Gloria   U2
Going Back to Gloria   Roy Orbison
Gloria   Erasure
Gloria   Doors

Grace

Amazing Grace   Judy Collins (and others)

The traditional spiritual has been recorded by saints and sinners everywhere for decades. The version by Judy Blue Eyes actually got AM airplay.

Of course, this song isn't about a *person*, but so what? Your daughter is *amazing,* isn't she?

OTHER ROCKIN' GRACE SONGS

State of Grace   Billy Joel
State of Grace   Steve Winwood
Your Saving Grace   Steve Miller

Grizelda
Your Auntie Grizelda   The Monkees

Guinnevere
Guinnevere   Crosby, Stills, and Nash

This pretty anthem by David Crosby is particularly fitting for a child with hazel eyes. "Guinnevere has green eyes," you can sing to her. "Like yours, m'baby, like yours."

Gus
Fifty Ways to Leave Your Lover   Paul Simon

Guy
Song for Guy   Elton John

Hank (see Henry)

Hannibal
    Hannibal   Santana

Harold
    Voice of Harold   R.E.M.

Harry
    Harry Truman   Chicago
    Harry's House   Joni Mitchell
    King Harry   John Cale
    Harry's Circumcision—Reverie Gone Astray   Lou Reed
    Harry   Janis Joplin
    Harry Rag   Kinks

Hattie
    Hurricane Hattie   Jimmy Cliff
    The Lonesome Death of Hattie Carroll   Bob Dylan

Hazel
    Hooray for Hazel   Tommy Roe
    Hazel   Bob Dylan

Heather
    Heather Honey   Tommy Roe

Hedda
    Hedda Gabler   John Cale

Heidi

Heidi is a Headache   Ramones

Your girl will have all kinds of effects on you. She'll make you proud, she'll fill you with joy, she'll make you crazy, she'll test your patience. Less known but just as universal is what she will do to your cranium: *she will give you splitting headaches.*

And during these times, you may just burst into a spontaneous chorus of this Ramones song. So name your girl Heidi.

Helen

Helen Wheels   Paul McCartney and Wings
Hey Hey Helen   ABBA
Helen of Troy   John Cale

Henry/Hank

I'm Henry VIII, I Am   Herman's Hermits
Love Henry   Bob Dylan (traditional)
From Hank to Hendrix   Neil Young
I Can't Reach You (Spotted Henry)   Who
Don't Ya Tell Henry   The Band
Henry's Swing Club   John Lee Hooker

Hercules

Hercules   Elton John

Hollis

The Ballad of Hollis Brown   Bob Dylan

Holly

Holly Holy   Neil Diamond

You may have started out a headbanger, a veteran of Black Sabbath concerts, and a devotee of Metallica. But having a baby can be a transforming experience. Upon welcoming your little girl into the world, you may just realize that this little creature is an *angel*. And those heavy metals riffs that have been banging around in your head for years might melt into the mellifluous sounds of Neil Diamond.

Or, you may have loved Neil Diamond all along and had

the same powerful reaction to parenthood. Either way, you might have a holy little Holly on your hands.

ANOTHER ROCKIN' HOLLY SONG

Holly Hop   Buddy Holly

Homer
Open the Door, Homer   Bob Dylan

Honey
Honey   Bobby Goldsboro

Igor

Igor's Boogie   Zappa/Mothers

Irene

Goodnight, Irene   Weavers (originally Leadbelly)

The classic version of this song (originally penned by the legendary Leadbelly) featured the seminal folk group The Weavers anxiously belting lyrics that were incredibly somber, even macabre, by fifties standards.

But forget the angst—it's still a good baby song. Chances are that from the time your girl is born, up until she pays her own rent, she's going to need coaxing to get some shut-eye. This song will do it. Talk to the clock-hands, Irene. Good-*night!*

Isabel

Isabel   John Denver

Isabella

Isabella's Eyes   Kenny Loggins
Izabella   Jimi Hendrix

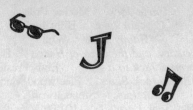

Jack

Jumpin' Jack Flash   Rolling Stones

For sheer exuberence and energy it's hard to top this Stones classic, a staple of their live show for decades. Mick Jagger used to take the jumping aspect quite seriously, and even in his fifties he's got a lot of hop left.

If your little bundle of jumpin' joy is destined to get physical, to pogo-dance, or be a trampoline artist, this is your name and your song.

It also might be useful for humoring yourself during times when your baby seems to be nothing but a breathing body function—after all, even the sweetest of little jumpin' Jacks will still get *gas gas gas*.

OTHER ROCKIN' JACK SONGS

Hit the Road, Jack   Ray Charles
Fifty Ways to Leave Your Lover   Paul Simon
Jack O'Diamonds   Bob Dylan
Jack and Diane   John Cougar Mellencamp
Jack and Jill   Raydio
Jack and Jill   Tommy Roe
Jackie Blue   Ozark Mountain Daredevils
Smackwater Jack   Carole King
Jack Straw   Grateful Dead
Jack-a-Roe   Grateful Dead/Bob Dylan (traditional)

> *Uncle Jack*   Mötley Crüe
> *Captain Jack*   Billy Joel
> *Happy Jack*   Who
> *Lily, Rosemary, and the Jack of Hearts*   Bob Dylan
> *From a Jack to a King*   Elvis Presley
> *Black Jack Blues*   Fleetwood Mac
> *Fat Jack*   Steppenwolf
> *Hey Jack Kerouac*   10,000 Maniacs
> *Wolfman Jack*   Todd Rundgren
> *The Return of Jackie and Judy*   Ramones
> *Jackie Wilson Said*   Van Morrison
> *Jack the Lad*   Pet Shop Boys
> *Jack*   AC/DC
> *Jack the Ripper*   John Cale
> *Jack D'or*   Deep Purple
> *Jack of all Parades*   Elvis Costello
> *Lumberjack*   Willie Nelson
> *Do it Again*   Steely Dan

Jackson

Jackson Cage   Bruce Springsteen
Jackson Kent Blues   Steve Miller

Jacob

Jacob's Ladder   Huey Lewis

Jake

Get Up Jake   The Band

If allowed, the average teenager will sleep until about two in the afternoon. Tests have shown, though, that a steady chorus of The Band's *Get Up Jake*, if sung persistently by both parents, will not only get him out of bed but have him out of the *house* by about 9 a.m.

James

Sweet Baby James   James Taylor

Some babies are sweeter than others (of course, yours is surely the sweetest). If you can't find enough sweet superlatives to express your baby's sweetness, this could be your song.

Like Paul Simon's *St. Judy's Comet*, this song is in the category of rockin' *chair* baby songs—that is, it's a lullaby, designed to induce sleep in one's sweet baby. With this song, one gets the feeling the baby's so sweet that the lullaby is a mere formality, sung for the sheer joy of it.

OTHER ROCKIN' JAMES SONGS

Jimmy Mack   Martha and the Vandellas
James (Hold the Ladder Steady)   Sue Thompson
Row Jimmy   Grateful Dead
James Dean   Eagles
James   Billy Joel
Jim Jones   Bob Dylan
Just Tell Her Jim Said Hello   Elvis Presley
Jimi   Beastie Boys
Jimmy James   Beastie Boys
Dr. Jimmy   Who
Top Jimmy   Van Halen
Captain Jim's Drunken Dream   James Taylor
James   Carly Simon
Plastic Jim   Sly and the Family Stone
Kristen and Jim   Rush
Jimmy Jimmy   Madonna
James   Bangles
Oh Jim   Lou Reed
James Dean   Eagles
Jimmy   Devo
Jesse James   John Lee Hooker
Jimmy's Road   Willie Nelson
I'm Bad Like Jesse James   John Lee Hooker

Jamie
Jamie   Ray Parker Jr.
Jamie   Jackson Five

Jane

Janie's Got a Gun   Aerosmith

Certainly you don't want to condone any violent behavior in your child; nonetheless, if you're a family that is, shall we say, rather *emotive* and likes to express its anger and keeps its NRA membership up-to-date—well, this could be a good tongue-in-cheek song for you.

It's also a good alternative if you had your heart set on *Careful with that Axe, Eugene* (*see* Eugene)—but had a girl.

OTHER ROCKIN' JANE SONGS

Sweet Jane   Lou Reed
Lady Jane   Rolling Stones
Baby Jane   Rod Stewart
Jane   Jefferson Starship
Queen Jane Approximately   Bob Dylan
Jane is a Groupie   Sly and the Family Stone
Me and Baby Jane   Leon Russell
Mary Jane's Last Dance   Tom Petty and The
                             Heartbreakers
Two Janes   Los Lobos
Sweet Jane   Velvet Underground
Liza Jane   David Bowie
Mary Jane   Rick James
Mary Jane   Janis Joplin

Janet

Go On Miss Janet   Janet Jackson

Janice

Ask For Janice   Beastie Boys
Sweet Jannie   Van Morrison

Jean/Jeannie
Little Jeannie   Elton John
Daydream Believer   Monkees

Two strong baby Jean candidates here. The Elton John tune is as good and sweet a baby song as any—for a little Jeannie you're *so* in love with.

The Monkees hit is a lullaby-in-reverse, a reverie of sorts—perfect for those times when you need to wake up your sleepy Jean. And this, of course, is useful not only for a baby, but for your teenaged Jean. ''Wake up, sleepy Jean,'' you can coax her when she's sixteen, on a Saturday—at two in the afternoon.

OTHER ROCKIN' JEAN NAMES

Blue Jean   David Bowie
Jean   Oliver
Jean Genie   David Bowie
The Ballad of Denny and Jean   Todd Rundgren
Mae Jean Goes to Hollywood   Byrds
Billy Jean   Michael Jackson
Candle in the Wind   Elton John

Jed
The Ballad of Jed Clampett   Flatt and Scruggs

It's not a rock song, really—it was written and performed by a pair of old-time banjo pickers. Still, endless reruns of this TV series about the changing fortunes of a poor mountaineer have left a permanent stamp on more than one rockin' generation. Even Beavis and Butt-head know about ''black gold and Texas tea.''

Can you picture your son with a perpetually torn hat, hayseed common sense, and long lucky streak? Then name him Jed, and thank him for kindly droppin' in.

Jeff
Jeff's Boogie   Yardbirds
Jeff's Blues   Clapton/Beck/Page
Susie and Jeffrey   Blondie

Jemima
Electric Aunt Jemima   Zappa/Mothers

Jennifer
867-5309 (Jenny)   Tommy Tutone

In the great tradition of song-immortalized phone numbers (such as *Pennsylvania 6-5000* by Glenn Miller and *Beechwood 4-5789* by the Marvelettes), Tommy Tutone branded a new number—867-5309—into the public consciousness in 1982 with this song (and its witty companion video).

We don't know too much about Jenny in this song except her phone number, with which the singer's obsessed. If you're bound to have a daughter who talks a lot on the phone and has boys clamoring for her number (the chances of this happening are approximately 99 percent), this could be your song.

Jennifer	Eurythmics
Jenny	Chicago

Jeremiah
Joy to the World   Three Dog Night
The Jeremiah Blues Part I   Sting

Jeremy
Jeremy   Pearl Jam

Jeremy's a nice name, and there are ways you can make Jeremy a rockin' baby name. Take the sixties duo, Chad and Jeremy, for instance. Harmless, clean cut. Now *there's* a Jeremy a mom would be proud of.

Then there's the Jeremy in the Pearl Jam grunge song, *Jeremy*, the kid everyone made fun of who got his revenge in a big way. *Surely* you don't want to name your boy after *this* Jeremy!

Jerome
Bring it to Jerome   Bo Diddley

Jesse
Whispering Jesse   John Denver
Jesse   Carly Simon
Jesse James   John Lee Hooker
I'm Bad Like Jesse James   John Lee Hooker

Jessica
Jessica   Allman Brothers

This song just goes to show you that not all baby name songs need to have lyrics. This classic Allman Brothers instrumental immortalizes the name Jessica without any of the vocalists uttering a peep.

Maybe you're a guitarist, a fan of the Allman sound, and this upbeat tune captures the spirit of your little girl. Why not?

Jessie
Jessie's Girl   Rick Springfield

You may have a boy who always gets the girl. And maybe he'll even have a girlfriend that's the envy of all his friends.

If so, consider him lucky and think about calling him Jessie.

ANOTHER ROCKIN' JESSIE SONG

Dear Jessie   Madonna

Jezebel
Jezebel   Sade
Jezebel   10,000 Maniacs
Jezebel Spirit   Brian Eno

Jill
Jack and Jill   Raydio

Jo
Jo's Lament   Rod Stewart

Jo Jo
Get Back   Beatles

As the Beatles were drifting apart, and the rift between John Lennon and Paul McCartney seemed to be spelled *Y-o-k-o*, Paul wrote this slightly veiled plea to John (''Jo Jo'') to coax him to ''get back,'' i.e., get his focus back on the Beatles and off of Ms. Ono.

Which, of course, has nothing to do with your baby. Still the song could work for you in many contexts. You're always going to need to tell your kid to ''get back''— whether he's going back to school, or back to his bedroom, or back in centerfield to catch a long fly.

Joan
Prelude to Joannie   Aerosmith
Joannie's Butterfly   Aerosmith
Come Back Jonee   Devo
Joan Crawford   Blue Oyster Cult

Joanna
Joanna   Kool and the Gang

No one wants your baby as much as you do, no one loves her as much, and no one could make you feel as fine as she does. So name her Joanna, after the Kool and the Gang song that's downright warm.

Jody
Jody Girl   Bob Seger
Papa Come Quick (Jody and Chico)   Bonnie Raitt
Jodie   Rod Stewart
Jody   Jeff Beck Group

John
Johnny B. Goode   Chuck Berry

There's no shortage of John songs to choose from—whether you've got a *Little John of God* or a *Big Bad John*.
    Chuck Berry's *Johnny B. Goode* song may be the most

55

widely known, and has been covered by groups from the Beach Boys to the Grateful Dead. If ever a song had a recurrent tag that will be useful to you as a parent, this is the one. Care to estimate the number of times you're going to say "Johnny, be good!" to your little boy? How about forty million!

OTHER ROCKIN' JOHN SONGS

Johnny Angel   Shelly Fabares
Bye Bye Johnny   Chuck Berry
Big Bad John   Jimmy Dean
Who's Johnny   El DeBarge
Sloop John B   Beach Boys (traditional)
Johnny Got Angry   Joannie Sommers
Long John Silver   Jefferson Airplane
Abraham, Martin, and John   Dion
Uncle John's Band   Grateful Dead
The Ballad of John and Yoko   Beatles
Bye Bye Johnny   Rolling Stones
St. John   Aerosmith
Dear John   Elton John
Empty Garden (Bye Bye Johnny)   Elton John
Johnny 99   Bruce Springsteen
Ghost of Tom Joad   Bruce Springsteen
John Wesley Harding   Bob Dylan
John Brown   Bob Dylan
Johnny Carson   Beach Boys
Farmer John   Neil Young and Crazy Horse
Johnny's Garden   Crosby, Stills, and Nash
I, John   Elvis Presley
Frankie and Johnny   Elvis Presley
Johnny Ryall   Beastie Boys
Johnny Are You Queer?   Go-Gos
When Johnnie Comes Back   James Taylor
The Late Great Johnny Ace   Paul Simon
Johnny, Kick a Hole in the   Red Hot Chili Peppers
Sky
Johnee Jingo   Todd Rundgren

> *Rave On, John Donne*   Van Morrison
> *John's Music Box*   Mamas and Papas
> *John Sinclair*   John Lennon
> *Little John of God*   Los Lobos
> *John Milton*   John Cale
> *Ballad of Spider John*   Jimmy Buffett
> *John Riley*   Byrds
> *Old John Robertson*   Byrds
> *Who Slapped John*   Jeff Beck and the Big Town
> Playboys
> *John, I'm Only Dancing*   David Bowie
> *It's Johnny's Birthday*   George Harrison
> *Johnny Says Come Back*   John Lee Hooker
> *Johnny Lee's Mood*   John Lee Hooker
> *Johnny Lee's Original Boogie*   John Lee Hooker
> *Johnny Lee and the Thing*   John Lee Hooker
> *One Was Johnny*   Carole King
> *Johnny Thunder*   Kinks

Jolie
Jolie   Roy Orbison

Jonah
Jonah   Paul Simon

Jordan
River Jordan   Janis Joplin

Joseph
Hey Joe   Jimi Hendrix (originally Leaves)

This song was played by about every act this side of Guy Lombardo in the late sixties—remarkable considering the original record was by an obscure East Coast group and got virtually no airplay. The enduring recording is the moderately paced Hendrix cut, which showcases his pearly-toned guitar.

The lyrics aren't typical baby name material. The subject of the song has been cuckolded, and is seeking a revenge that could get him the chair. Still, the tune has potential if you fudge the words a little. "Hey Joe," you can sing to your mischievous boy, "where you goin' with that cookie jar in your hand?" You get the idea.

OTHER ROCKIN' JOSEPH SONGS

Joe Hill   Joan Baez
Run Joey Run   David Geddes
Joey   Bob Dylan
Diamond Joe   Bob Dylan
Tequila Joe   Bob Dylan
I'm Tired, Joey Boy   Van Morrison
Joe Harper Saturday Morning   Van Morrison
Stay Away, Joe   Elvis Presley
Joe the Lion   David Bowie
Smokey Joe's Café   Buddy Holly

Josephine
My Girl Josephine   Fats Domino
Ride On Josephine   Bo Diddley

Joshua
Joshua Fit (Fought) the Battle of Jericho   Elvis Presley

This unlikely song (adapted from a theme by composer Edvard Grieg) offers a fun, repetitive tune that you can sing over and over to your child, particularly if he's a spunky, combative little tyke.

And for a twist, you can sing the Allan Sherman parody of the tune, the title of which tells it all: *Jasha Bought a Bottle of Geritol*.

ANOTHER JOSHUA ROCKER

Joshua Tree (album)   U2

Josie
Josie   Steely Dan

Seize the opportunity—this is one of the few Steely Dan numbers with lyrics that follow an understandable narrative (relatively speaking).

In any case, assuming it's always going to be "so good" when she comes home—from the hospital, from her first day at school, from summer camp, from college—then you can have an ongoing anthem in Josie.

After all, like this song's Josie, your child is the pride of the neighborhood, isn't she?

Joy
Joy to the World   Three Dog Night

You can't go wrong with this classic happy-rocker, which should be fun to sing with your little girl for years to come. With this song, you can teach her to sing, to dance, to do jumping-jacks.

It'll work all the better if you have an aquarium in your home, and she can appreciate the joy of the fishes in your clear blue fish tank.

OTHER ROCKIN' JOY SONGS

Joy   Apollo 100
A Song of Joy   Miguel Rios
Joy to the World   Four Seasons
Joy (Takes Over Me)   Stevie Wonder
Joy in Repetition   Prince
Only Joy in Town   Joni Mitchell
Joy to Have You Home   Labelle

Joyce
Rejoyce   Jefferson Airplane

Judas
Judas   Depeche Mode

Jude
Hey Jude   Beatles

Sometime along the way you'll have to talk you child out of being miserable, whether he (or she) is a baby bawling over something trivial, or a teenager who's been unlucky in love. In which case you can tell your Jude not to "take it bad."

Other kids might taunt your child with this song, though, so be warned. "Nyah, nyah, nyah nyah-nyah-nyah-nyah!" they might sing to the long fade, which could be annoying.

Trivia: *Hey Jude* was Paul McCartney's attempt to console young Julian Lennon, whose dad, John Lennon, had left his mother for Yoko Ono.

Judy
St. Judy's Comet   Paul Simon

There are more famous Judy songs, but none better for a baby than the gorgeous *St. Judy's Comet*, written expressly *for* a baby by the then newly parental Paul Simon. A lullaby, it's actually written for a boy, but it doesn't have to be sung that way.

A little Judy influenced by this song will be in awe of celestial wonders, of diamond-sparkling comets. A lovely sentiment, a lovely song.

OTHER ROCKIN' JUDY SONGS

Suite: Judy Blue Eyes	Crosby, Stills, and Nash
Judy in Disguise (with Glasses)	John Ford and His Playboy Band
Judy's Turn to Cry	Leslie Gore
Judy	Beach Boys
Why Judy Why	Billy Joel
Judy	Elvis Presley
Jewel Eyed Judy	Fleetwood Mac

> *Judy is a Punk*   Ramones
> *The Return of Jackie and Judy*   Ramones
> *Back in Judy's Jungle*   Brian Eno
> *Miss Judy's Farm*   Faces
> *Judy*   Al Green

Julia
Julia   Beatles

This earnest song, a remarkably peaceful moment for John Lennon, expresses a tender love. It's one of the prettiest Lennon songs ever, and if you've got a tender, earnest, sensitive little girl, this one could be for you. It's so quiet it could almost be a lullaby.

There's a tinge of sadness, even angst, in this song, for good reason. The real-life subject of *Julia* was Lennon's mother, who was chronically ill and absent from most of his childhood.

ANOTHER ROCKIN' JULIA SONG

Julia Dream   Pink Floyd

Julie
Julie Do You Love Me   Bobby Sherman
Julie Through the Glass   Carly Simon
Julie   Brian Eno

Juliet
Romeo and Juliet   Dire Straits

If you think you have a little streetside serenadee on your hands, consider *Romeo and Juliet* by Dire Straits.

Julio
Me and Julio Down By the Schoolyard   Paul Simon

Granted, the song is about some no-no going on in a schoolyard, but you don't have to dwell on that. This could be the anthem for an academic-minded little Julio—me and Julio on his first day of nursery school, or kindergarten or college. It's not against the law.

June
Junebug   B-52s

Junior
Junior's Farm   Paul McCartney and Wings

Kathleen

Kathy's Song Simon and Garfunkel
Kathleen (Catholicism Made Easier) Randy Newman
Kathleen's Song Byrds

Katie

Katy Lied Steely Dan

It's possible you'll have one of those virtuous children who, after you find your cherry tree's been chopped down, will tell you, "Mother, Father: I cannot tell a lie. It was I who . . ."—you get the idea.

On the other hand, and more likely, you may come home one day to find your entire cherry orchard cut down, and the only clue to what happened is that your devilish little daughter smells like a buzz saw. And she may look you straight in the eye, shrug, and say, "I didn't do it."

So Katy, in the Steely Dan sense, may be a good name for your girl. *Realistic*, certainly.

OTHER ROCKIN' KATIE SONGS

Katie Mae Grateful Dead
Katie's Been Gone Bob Dylan

Katrina
  Katrina's Fair   10,000 Maniacs

Kayleigh
  Kayleigh   Marillion

Kelly
  Machine Gun Kelly   James Taylor

Kent
  Jackson Kent Blues   Steve Miller

Kerry
  Kerry   Hall and Oates

A fun song by Hall and Oates, which offers a pun: this
Kerry is inclined to get "carried away." Your little girl
may be prone to this, whether she's throwing a tantrum or
getting giddy or exaggerating a blue streak. So name her
Kerry and you can always have a song to gently rib her
about it.

Kevin
  Cousin Kevin   Who

Kiko
  Kiko and the Lavender Moon   Los Lobos

Kitty
  Kitty's Back   Bruce Springsteen

Kristen
  Kristen and Jim   Rush

Kurt
  Kurt's Rejoinder   Brian Eno

Kyrie
  Kyrie   Mr. Mister

Lahaina
Lahaina Loggins and Messina

Lana
Lana Beach Boys
Lana Roy Orbison

Larry
Hats Off to Larry Del Shannon

Del Shannon's second most famous song (after *Runaway*) features a twist: the singer is singing Larry's praises because he managed to break the heart of the young woman who once broke the *singer's* heart—therefore, they're even. Get it?

Your little boy is no doubt chock full o' charm. Face it, unless you have an iron will, he'll be manipulating the heck out of you before he's a year old. And then, when he's older, leaving a trail of broken hearts.

So name him Lawrence, call him Larry, and take your hat off to him.

ANOTHER ROCKIN' LARRY SONG

Larry the Logger Two-Step Doobie Brothers

Laura

Tell Laura I Love Her   Ray Peterson
Laura   Billy Joel
I'll See You On the Radio (Laura)   Neil Diamond

Layla

Layla   Derek and the Dominos

Perhaps you think *you're* in control of what your daughter is going to do once she's up and about. Ha! More likely, you're have to cajole her into doing what you want her to. Let's face it, you're going to need to get "on your knees." So, to face the next twenty-or-so years of pleading and bargaining, consider *Layla*, and you'll at least have an anthem for this dirty business.

Trivia: Layla was a fake name for George Harrison's wife, Patti, with whom Eric Clapton was smitten in the early seventies. *Layla* expresses his feeling of desperation and hopelessness when she was still married to George. Patti later, in fact, dumped George for Eric, temporarily getting Eric off of his knees—only to dump *him* still later.

Leah

Leah   Roy Orbison

Like most folks, you may be on a tight budget, struggling to make ends meet—but you still have big romantic dreams in your heart, and you want only nice things for your little daughter. Are you willing, for instance, to dive deep in oyster-rich waters for your little girl, seeking pearls to make her a pretty necklace?

Strange as it may sound, you wouldn't be the first. So consider *Leah*, after the Roy Orbison ballad, and you'll forever have someone for whom you'll go to the ends of the earth.

Lee

Stagger Lee   Lloyd Price

When your little Lee is about twelve months old, he is bound to occasionally resemble someone who's had a few too many. In which case *Stagger Lee* (covered by a few million groups, especially the Grateful Dead) may be a fitting name for him.

Trivia: *Stagger Lee* has a long history, and is actually based on a murder that took place in St. Louis in 1895. The original record, by Archibald (Leon T. Gross), dates from 1950 and featured violent lyrics. Even Lloyd Prices's catchy version had to be rerecorded with tame lyrics after Dick Clark refused to promote the original version on "American Bandstand."

OTHER ROCKIN' LEE SONGS

Fifty Ways to Leave Your Lover   Paul Simon
Lee Shore   Crosby, Stills, and Nash
Baby Lee   John Lee Hooker
Johnny Lee's Mood   John Lee Hooker
Johnny Lee's Original Boogie   John Lee Hooker
Johnny Lee and the Thing   John Lee Hooker

Leila

Leila   ZZ Top

Lenny

Lenny Bruce   Bob Dylan

Leroy
Bad Bad Leroy Brown   Jim Croce

Most children have a mischievous streak—some are even *bad*. And some kids are not just *bad*, they're *baaaaaad*. And some are not just *baaaaaad*, they're—well, you get the idea.

If you think it's good to be good, but better to be bad, consider Leroy and this bad bad song by Jim Croce. We're talking badness of a caliber exceeding King Kong—and let's face it, that's *bad*.

Lester
Looking for Lester   David Bowie

Leyna
All for Leyna   Billy Joel

Libby
Libby   Carly Simon

Lily
Dixie Lily   Elton John
Lily, Rosemary, and the Jack of Hearts   Bob Dylan
Lili's Address   Todd Rundgren
Lilly (Are You Happy?)   Hall and Oates

Linda
Lovely Linda   Paul McCartney and Wings

This song is about the late Linda McCartney, wife of Paul, but it could just as easily be about your baby. It's a retro flower-power anthem about a Linda who looks lovely with flowers in her hair. You can imagine flowers in your girl's hair, right? And she's lovely, right? Well, then it's perfect.

OTHER ROCKIN' LINDA SONGS

Linda   Randy Newman
Linda Lu   Ray Sharpe
Lady Lynda   Beach Boys

Lisa
I'm Not Lisa   Jessi Colter
Lisa Says   Velvet Underground

Liz (*see* Elizabeth)

Liza
Liza Jane   David Bowie

Lodi
Lodi   Creedence Clearwater Revival

Lois
Ballad of Lois Malone   Atlanta Rhythm Section

Lola
Lola   Kinks

Let's ignore, for the time being, the actual subject matter of this song. It's still got a catchy refrain, and it's a name that rhymes with all kinds of fun things. Your little Lo-lo-lo-lo-Lola may just be a fan of, say, *Cherry Cola*.

Be wary of that subject matter, though. And don't cross-dress your child.

ANOTHER ROCKIN' LOLA SONG

Frank and Lola   Jimmy Buffett

Lolita
Don't Stand So Close to Me   Police

Lorenzo
Lorenzo   Phil Collins

Lorraine
Lorraine   Toto
Quiche Lorraine   B-52s
Lorriane   Kenny Loggins

Louis
Louie Louie   Kingsmen

A terrific song of the post-Elvis, pre-Beatles period. It's a good rocker, and it has that great hook refrain—"Louie Louie." There's no doubt who this song is about.

Unfortunately, all of the other lyrics are completely indecipherable. In fact, it's hard to predict the destiny of a little Louie from this song, because the lyrics, sung by the Kingsmen as if they have cotton in their mouths, offer no clue. They might as well be in Hungarian.

Trivia: Radio censors, when this record was new, were not so convinced that the lyrics were indecipherable—or even benign. The song was banned on some stations because it allegedly contained an f-word (of all things). The buzz about this was, of course, great for record sales. Kids all over the land bought the 45s and wore them out trying to find the f-word. A futile exercise: they couldn't understand *any* of the lyrics.

OTHER ROCKIN' LOUIS SONGS

Brother Louie   Stories
Louisiana Lou and Three   Allman Brothers
Card Monty John
Louie Louie Go Home   David Bowie

Louise
Louise   Bonnie Raitt

Cherokee Louise   Joni Mitchell
Louise   Yardbirds
Louise   John Lee Hooker

Lucille/Lucy
Lucy in the Sky with Diamonds   Beatles

It will probably be debated forever whether or not this John Lennon opus is about *drugs* (particularly the hallucinogen implied by the title's initials). If you can put that matter aside, it's still a great rockin' baby name song.

What baby—or little girl—would *not* want to be a Lucy in the sky with diamonds? You can even install a disco ball in Lucy's room and twirl her high in the "sky" as the stars float by. You can take her to the planetarium, or just outside on a summer night, star-gazing . . . There are infinite possibilities for your little celestial wonder.

OTHER ROCKIN' LUCILLE SONGS

Lucille   Little Richard
Lucille   Kenny Rogers
Loose Lucy   Grateful Dead
Bring on the Lucie (Freeda People)   John Lennon
Lucille   Deep Purple
Watch Out for Lucy   Eric Clapton
Lucy Can't Dance   David Bowie
Letter to Lucille   Tom Jones

Lucifer
Lucifer Sam   Pink Floyd

Lucinda
Lucinda   Randy Newman

Luther
Dr. Luther's Assistant   Elvis Costello and the
                            Attractions

Mack

Mack the Knife Bobby Darin

Sometimes hit songs come from unlikely sources. As originally written by Kurt Weill and Bertoldt Brecht, *Mack the Knife* (*Mackie Messer*) was a street-singer ballad chronicling the illicit life of a small-time gangster in between-the-wars Germany. The lyrics were violent and macabre.

Somehow all of this was transformed into a swingin' cabaret vehicle for Bobby Darin (who recorded some rock 'n' roll records but always kept a foot firmly planted in Vegas). The modified lyrics still hint at violence, but segue into show-biz references—and as a whole make no sense.

Baby name? Well, why not? It *is* the quintessential lounge-lizard song, after all. And if your baby has evil little pearly-whites and looks like he should be wearing a fedora and a trenchcoat, and holding a revolver in his pocket—well, then this is your song!

Madonna

Lady Madonna Beatles

You can approach this name, and the song, from many angles.

First, there's an obvious religious angle. Then, of course, if you want to honor pop music's Evita, naming your girl after this song is one way to do it.

And if you're a Brett Butler fan, you'll remember that a

cover version of Lady Madonna was the theme song for "Grace Under Fire."

Finally, you may just like the Beatles and this song and the name. Whatever reason you like Madonna, go for it!

Mae

Miss Sadie Mae   John Lee Hooker
Stella Mae   John Lee Hooker
Sally Mae   John Lee Hooker
Dazie Mae   John Lee Hooker
Annie Mae   John Lee Hooker

If you like the name Mae, and you like John Lee Hooker, you're in luck: not only are there five songs to choose from, but five first names.

OTHER ROCKIN' MAE SONGS

Fanny Mae   Steve Miller
Mae Jean Goes to Hollywood   Byrds
Rita Mae   Eric Clapton

Magdalena

Magdalena   Zappa/Mothers
Magdalene Laundries   Joni Mitchell

Maggie

Maggie May   Rod Stewart

The subject matter—a student with an older woman—may not be exactly fitting for your little Maggie. But given how famous the song is (Rod's personal fave), and that one line implores Maggie to wake up, it may work for you. Because wake-up songs are always useful, from her baby days to when she's a teenager sleeping through the afternoon.

Magnolia
Sugar Magnolia   Grateful Dead

If you want to keep the spirit of the Summer of Love alive—and there are still a few million of you out there—you may want a name that evokes the sunny, flowery, peace and love, make love not war sentiment of the San Francisco scene of the late sixties. Magnolia, after the upbeat Dead song, is the perfect name for such a girl.

All the more true if you have a little girl who's destined to be a sixties-style dancer. Make sure you compliment her when she "jumps like a Willys"—of course, she'll have no idea what you're talking about.

Marcella
Marcella   Beach Boys

Marcie
Marcie   Joni Mitchell

Maria
Maria   Various (from *West Side Story*)

If you're a die-hard romantic, the kind who loves the sheer *sound* of your daughter's name, you may opt for Maria, after the Bernstein-Sondheim classic from *West Side Story*.

As far as singing this song goes, you may or may not be up for this. If you are a trained tenor—more than a shower-stall tenor—this could be a good one to sing to your daughter. Otherwise, use extreme caution. If you're a *bad* singer, a shower-stall belter, you might end up making your daughter long for outdoor plumbing.

OTHER ROCKIN' MARIA SONGS

My Maria   B. W. Stevenson
Take a Letter, Maria   R. B. Greaves
Ave Maria   Stevie Wonder
Sarah Maria   James Taylor
Maria Caracoles   Santana
Bella Maria de Mi Alma   Los Lobos
Maria (You Were the Only One)   Michael Jackson

Marianne
C'mon Marianne   Four Seasons

This song by the Four Seasons not only provides an alternate spelling of Mary Ann, it gives you an all-purpose prodding song ("c'mon!"), suitable for just about any occasion. "C'mon, Marianne!" you can plead to your girl, to get her to take her first steps, eat lima beans, stay away from your CD player, do her homework, get off the front porch with that pesky boyfriend of hers. There will *never* be a shortage of these situations.

Marie
His Latest Flame   Elvis Presley

There will come a time when your adorable, innocent daughter starts dating, but, of course, it won't be like any of the dating *you* did. You only dated nice people, but this daughter of yours, lovely and sweet as she is, may just start hanging out with someone who looks like he should be convicted, or committed.

So you might find yourself in a situation akin to The King's feelings for his Marie in *His Latest Flame*. Not to confuse romantic jealousy with parental feelings, but you may find that as your little girl grows up and moves on that it feels, well, tragic.

OTHER ROCKIN' MARIE SONGS

Marie   Randy Newman
Absolutely Sweet Marie   Bob Dylan
Little Marie   Chuck Berry
Sweet Marie   Loggins and Messina

Marjorine
Marjorine   Joe Cocker

Marlena
Marlena   Four Seasons

Marlene
Marlene   Todd Rundgren

Marlon
Goodbye Marlon Brando   Elton John

Martha
Martha My Dear   Beatles

You may just have a silly girl, who needs to hold her head up. At the age of a few months, that may be a physical challenge, and later, the emotional one we all deal with. So name your dear girl after this classic Beatles tune.

Martin
Abraham, Martin, and John   Dion

Mary
Proud Mary   Creedence Clearwater Revival

There are lots of Mary songs, but none more famous—or more fun—than *Proud Mary*. It was first sung first by Creedence Clearwater Revival—but there are great covers, particularly by Ike and Tina Turner, with Tina, as usual, singing her heart out.

If you've got a self-possessed, confident, struttin' little girl, this is a great song for you. With this song as her anthem and dance theme, she'll be "rollin', rollin', rollin' " through whatever ails her.

Mary-Anne
Mary-Anne with the Shaky Hands   Who

Mandy
Mandy   Barry Manilow

Parenthood may be so overwhelming blissful to you that you feel like your little joy is actually giving without taking. (If you don't feel this way, don't fret it.) If it's so overwhelming that you need your little precious to kiss you to stop you from shaking, well, name her Mandy and belt out the Manilow number.

Matilda
Tom Traubert's Blues (Waltzing Matilda)   Rod Stewart

Matthew
Matthew   John Denver

Maude
Maudie   John Lee Hooker

Maureen
Maureen   Sade

Maxine
Sweet Maxine   Doobie Brothers

Maxwell
Maxwell's Silver Hammer   Beatles

Maybellene
Maybellene   Chuck Berry

Melissa
Melissa   Allman Brothers
Sweet Little Missy   Lynyrd Skynyrd

Sure, all babies are sweet, and yours is, of course, the
sweetest. (Why, if it weren't for babies, words like *sweet*
wouldn't even have to exist.) In the case of Melissa (and
its nickname Missy) there are two strong songs to express
the sweetness of your little girl.

Mia
Mama Mia   ABBA

You never know: your little Mia, amazing as she is, may
just cause you to exclaim, "Mama!"
    How can you resist her?

OTHER ROCKIN' MIA SONGS

Mia   Aerosmith
Mea Culpa   Brian Eno

Michael
Michael   Highwaymen
Mikey's   Randy Newman
Message To Michael   Dionne Warwick
Michael From Mountains   Joni Mitchell

Michelle
Michelle   Beatles

The oh-so-sophisticated Paul McCartney came up with this ballad, and back in 1966 sweethearts held their transistor radios and each other to this tune.

And it's a perfectly sweet baby-name tune. Your Michelle will be elegant and serene, if she takes after this song, with a bent toward translating everything into French.

OTHER ROCKIN' MICHELLE SONGS

Michelle's Farm   Beastie Boys
My Michelle   Al Green

Mickey
Mickey   Toni Basil

Milton
John Milton   John Cale

Miranda
Crazy Miranda   Jefferson Starship

Missy (*see* Melissa)

Mo
Is That You Mo—Dean?   B-52s

Molina
Molina   Creedence Clearwater Revival

Molly
Good Golly Miss Molly   Little Richard

Good Golly, this is a fun rockin' baby song. For a fun-lovin', joy-jumpin' little Molly, there couldn't be a better song. You can teach you girl to dance, to laugh, to smile, and to sing with this song. She'll be lovin' life.

ANOTHER ROCKIN' MOLLY SONG

Molly   John Denver

Mona
Mona   Rolling Stones (originally Bo Diddley)
Mona   Beach Boys
Mona Lisas and Mad Hatters   Elton John
Mona   James Taylor
Mona Lisa Please   Leon Russell
Mona   Bo Diddley
Mona Lisa   Willie Nelson

Monica
Monica   Kinks

Monty
Louisiana Lou and Three   Allman Brothers
Card Monty John

Morris
Morris' Nightmare   Jimmy Buffett
Mighty Morris Ten   Deep Purple

Nadia
Nadia's Theme   Barry DeVorzon and
(The Young and the Restless)   Perry Botkin

Nadine
Nadine (Is It You)   Chuck Berry

Chuck Berry, God bless him, managed to write the best rock 'n' roll baby name songs. Thank you, Chuck!
    Nadine is the perfect peek-a-boo song, when you're teaching your little infant to respond to you—your voice, your eyes, her name.

Napoleon
Poor Napoleon   Elvis Costello

Nathan
Nathan Jones   Supremes
Nathan La Franeer   Joni Mitchell

Neal
Neal's Fandango   Doobie Brothers

Negrita
Hey Negrita   Rolling Stones

Nellie (*see* Eleanor)

Nemo
Little Nemo in Nightland   Grateful Dead

Nick
Nick of Time   AC/DC

Nikita
Nikita   Elton John

Nikki
Darling Nikki   Prince

Warning! If you name your child after this song, you may just get a *personal* visit (and admonition) from Tipper Gore!

Noah
Noah's Dove   10,000 Maniacs

Nona
Nona   Mötley Crüe

Norma Jean
Candle in the Wind   Elton John

Norman
Norman   Sue Thompson

If you remember this song, which is rarely heard today (even on oldies stations), you may well be shopping for rockin' *grand*-baby names. No matter. This song is a lot of fun, Ms. Thompson's confident expression of fidelity for Norman, back when putting one's object of affection on a pedestal was considered a high form of love.

If you're just bursting with love for your little boy, consider Norman. This kissin', huggin', lovey-dovin' song isn't for everybody, but for a love that borders on smothering, it's perfect.

Oliver
Oliver's Army   Elvis Costello and the Attractions
Rock Around with Ollie Vee   Buddy Holly

Ophelia
Ophelia   The Band

Orpheus
Orpheus   Carly Simon

Otis
Muddy, Sam, and Otis   Rod Stewart

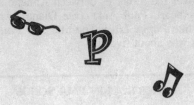

Pamela
Polythene Pam   Beatles
Pamela   Toto

Pandora
Pandora's Box   Aerosmith

Parker
Parker's Band   Steely Dan

Pat
Pat Garrett and Billy the Kid   Bob Dylan

Paul
Tall Paul   Annette Funicello

Oh, all right—yes, this kind of song makes even most sentimental folk want to gak these days. But keep in mind that most people, even those who start out cooler than cool, find themselves doing things like singing "Itsy Bitsy Spider" in shrill, scary voices once they have an infant. So maybe having a baby song by a mouseketeer isn't such a bad thing.

You may have one of those babies who's born with all legs. In fact, babies who start out that way often end up looking like Kareem. Your boy may even like the song *Tall Paul*; if you make fun of it, he may well look (down) at you and tell you to show some respect, in which case you'll look back at him and say, "Yes, sir!"

Trivia: *Tall Paul* was one of a few cutsie songs exchanged over the airwaves between Annette and her teen-aged sweetheart, Paul Anka (*see* Diana), who countered with hits like *Puppy Love*. The title *Tall Paul* was ironic; Mr. Anka was about five-six.

OTHER ROCKIN' PAUL SONGS

Slippery St. Paul   Doobie Brothers
Me and Paul   Willie Nelson

Paula
Hey, Paula   Paul and Paula

Pearl
Black Pearl   Sonny Charles / Checkmates Ltd.
Pearl of the Quarter   Steely Dan
Pearly Queen   Steve Winwood
Pearl   Tommy Roe
Pearl   Stevie Wonder
Mama's Pearl   Jackson Five
Diamonds and Pearls   Prince
Pearl   Brian Eno
Pearly Queen   Eric Clapton
Apologies to Pearly   ZZ Top

Peggy
Peg   Steely Dan
Peggy Sue   Buddy Holly

Who knows (as usual) what's up with the Steely Dan tune—something having to do with a model, having pictures made . . . who knows. Still, with the ever-repeating "Peg" refrain, it's a strong rockin' baby name song. And if you're shutterbug parents, and your Peg is a flirt with the camera, then it's perfect.

Less complicated (to put it mildly) in content and sentiment is the classic Buddy Holly song. If you have a love for your little Peggy Sue that's rare and true, it's irresistible.

Penny
Penny Lane   Beatles

Penny is the name for you if you want to name your girl after what some consider the best double-sided single of all time (it'll have to be Penny, because you're probably not going to find a name in *Strawberry Fields Forever*).

Penny makes sense as a name too, especially if you live under those fine suburban skies, and you have a girl who's forever in your ears and in your eyes. Most babies are.

Percy
Percy's Song   Bob Dylan

Peter
Black Peter   Grateful Dead
Peter Gunn   Emerson, Lake, and Palmer

Petunia
Petunia, the Gardener's Daughter   Elvis Presley

Pierre
Pierre in Mist   Brian Eno

Pinky
   Pinky   Elton John

Polly
   Polly   Nirvana
   Pretty Polly   Byrds
   Polly   Kinks

Priscilla
   Priscilla   Eddie Cooley

Prudence
   Dear Prudence   Beatles

Name your girl Prudence, and persistent, whiny guys will forever be trying to ask her out by crooning this song. And once they get her out, they'll continue their whining, trying to break her resistance.

As a parent, you may be inclined to lock her in the house if all this is going on. No need! After all, her name is *Prudence*.

Trivia: Rumor has it this song is about an experience John Lennon had while the Beatles were in Marrakesh with various celebrities and Maharishi Mahesh Yogi. While seeking inner peace and enlightenment, John Lennon apparently was distracted by the charms of another truth-searcher, Prudence Farrow (sister of Mia), whose rebuffs inspired him to write *Dear Prudence*.

Quentin
Quentin's Theme   Charles Randolph

Rachel

Little Rachel   Eric Clapton

Ramona

To Ramona   Bob Dylan
Ramona   Ramones

Ray

Celtic Ray   Van Morrison
Ray of Sunshine   Wham!
Sister Ray   Velvet Underground

Rene

Rene and Georgette Magritte   Paul Simon
with their Dog After the War

Renee

Walk Away, Renee   Left Banke

A sad little tune, performed by the five teenaged college dropouts who spawned the genre ''baroque rock,'' which lasted for about five minutes in 1966.

It's a pretty good baby song, though, for a peripatetic little Renee. *Walk Away, Renee*, you can coax your little girl as she takes her first baby steps. *Walk Away, Renee*, you can tell her when she's older and is misbehaving at the dinner table. And *Walk Away, Renee,* you can inform her—by way of giving notice—if she's still living at home at *age thirty*.

Reva

Reva's House   Los Lobos

Rhiannon

Rhiannon (Will You Ever Win)   Fleetwood Mac

You may have one of those lovable little screwups, and if it's a boy you may want to name your child after the Coasters hit *Charlie Brown* (*see* Charles).

For a girl, Rhiannon may be your tune, for the girl who's graced with a long streak of bad luck.

Rhonda

Help Me, Rhonda/Ronda   Beach Boys

The only Billboard #1 baby name hit by the surfin' serenaders. (The group also went all the way with *I Get Around*, *Good Vibrations*, and *Kokomo*, but when it comes to naming your child, what good are *they*?) *Rhonda* is quintessential Boys: catchy and happy—even though it's about someone trying to distract himself out of heartache.

This song could come in handy as your little Rhonda is growing up. *Help Me, Rhonda* could be the anthem you sing to her whenever you need any domestic assistance—with the dishes, the lawn, the vacuuming, or cleaning up her darn room! (And hearing it sung to her on such occasions is something she will *never* tire of!)

Trivia: The Boys recorded this song twice, which accounts for the variant spellings. *Help Me, Ronda* came first, as non-hit album filler; then the number was recut in a crisper version for the single release. The second effort paid off big for the group.

Richard/Dick

Moby Dick   Led Zeppelin
Song for Richard and His Friends   Chicago

Ricky

Ricky's Theme   Beastie Boys

Rico

Rico Suave   Gerardo

Rikki

Rikki Don't Lose That Number   Steely Dan

One of the many great jazzy top-forty singles by Steely Dan. Like most of their songs, the lyrics aren't exactly straightforward—in fact, the meaning of this song is probably known only to a few stoners scattered here and there. (And they're not talking.)

Still, the oft-repeated refrain could apply to endless situations for you and your little girl. *Rikki, Don't Lose That Number!* you can say to her as she goes to her first sleepover, and you're comforted by the knowledge that she is only a phone call away. *Rikki, Don't Lose That Number!* you can implore her, as you send her out to get your Lottery tickets. And *Rikki, Don't Lose That Number!* you can nag her, when she's thirty and living at home, as you send her off with her social security number to get a job!

If you have a boy, you can adapt the song to "Ricky"—or, believe if or not, you can name him Billy, after *another* number-losing song (*see* William).

Ringo

Ringo   Lorne Greene

Back in the days when the Beatles vied for top-forty airtime with middle-aged performers like Dean Martin and Louis Armstrong, this extremely unlikely tune managed to be a big hit. Sung—spoken, really—by Lorne Greene, portrayer of Paw Cartwright on "Bonanza" and hawker of Alpo, the song was a parody of Jimmy Dean's *Big Bad John*, focusing on the Beatle who at that time tended to be ridiculed by everyone other than teenaged girls.

If you want to name a child after a Beatle (and there's none nicer than Mr. Starr), it's good to know there's a baby song even for good ol' Ringo.

Rita

Lovely Rita   Beatles

It's a given that your little girl is not just cute, or adorable, or beautiful—but she's absolutely *lovely*. Which makes

Rita a good name candidate—name her Rita, and there's a lovely song with her name on it.

So what is little lovely Rita destined to become in her lovely life? Well, she could take her cue from this song and become . . . a meter maid! Not the most glamorous job in the world, but at least it's steady!

ANOTHER ROCKIN' RITA SONG

Rita Mae　　Eric Clapton

Robert
Bobby's Girl　　Marcie Blane
Abraham, Martin, and John　　Dion
Me and Bobby McGee　　Janis Joplin (originally Kris Kristofferson)
Dr. Robert　　Beatles
Uncle Bob's Midnight Blues　　Randy Newman
Bob George　　Prince
Me and Bobby and Bobby's Brother　　ABBA
Song for Bob Dylan　　David Bowie

Roberta
Roberta　　Billy Joel

Robin
Fly Robin Fly　　Silver Connection
Rockin' Robin　　Michael Jackson (originally Bobby Day)

Robin is such a good rockin' baby name! Not only are there two strong Robin songs in catalog, but either of them can be used with a boy *or* a girl.

The classic *Rockin' Robin* not only teaches your child to rock but is a good tutorial for bird sounds. Can you say "tweedley-deedley-dee" three times, fast?

And if there's an aviator in your baby, what better tune than *Fly Robin Fly*? You can fly your baby around to this tune—right up to the sky.

Rocky

Rocky Raccoon   Beatles
Rocky   Austin Roberts

If you've got a little rockin' Rocky, there are two strong candidates for his rockin' theme song, and they're very different.

The Beatles tune, which features Paul McCartney singing far afield in a hillbilly accent, is fitting for your child if you have a gold ole (baby) boy on your hands.

The movie-music tune, an atypical hit from the movie of the same name, will work for a little champion, especially a pugilist who's "feelin' strong."

OTHER ROCKIN' ROCKY SONGS

Loves Me Like a Rock   Paul Simon
Rocky Mountain Breakdown   Poco
Rocky Mountain High   John Denver

Romeo

Romeo and Juliet   Dire Straits

The complement to Juliet. If you think you have a little streetside serenader on your hands, consider *Romeo and Juliet* by Dire Straits.

OTHER ROCKIN' ROMEO SONGS

Romeo   Dion
Romeo's Tune   Steve Forbert
(Just Like) Romeo and Juliet   Reflections
Romeo Delight   Van Halen

> *Romeo and Juliet*   Lou Reed
> *Romeo and Juliet*   Emerson, Lake, and Palmer

Ronnie
Ronnie   Four Seasons
Ronnie, Talk to Russia   Prince

Rosalie
Rosalie McFall   Grateful Dead

Rosalinda
Rosalinda's Eyes   Billy Joel

Are there Cuban skies in your little girl's eyes? She may just be a Rosalinda.

Rosalita
Rosalita (Come Out Tonight)   Bruce Springsteen

Springsteen's classic tells the story of a young man's despaired attempt to meet his beloved (that would be Rosalita), in spite of her parents' disapproval, a scenario bound to happen with your little girl, too. When your Rosalita starts shimmying down fire escapes to escape your watchful eye, you'll be recalling this anthem by the Boss, wishing you could teach *her* who's boss.

Rosalyn
Rosalyn   David Bowie

Rosanna
Rosanna   Toto

A great perky little tune, perfect for a little one-year-old's two-step. Imagine your little daughter's hands in yours as you teach her to dance, swaying her gently and singing *Rosanna* to her. It's so adorable.

Trivia: This song was written about actress Rosanna Arquette, who dated band member Steve Porcaro in the early eighties. Porcaro didn't write it though; his band-mate David Paich did, in appreciation of Ms. Arquette, who cheerfully brought the group juice and beer in the wee hours as they recorded albums.

Rose
Cracklin' Rosie   Neil Diamond

It's unlikely that your girl is, as the song says, "store-bought" (there aren't too many baby stores in these parts), but she might embody the famous Neil Diamond tune in some other way. It could be a good song for encouraging a taciturn little girl to talk; you can encourage her over and over to "say it now."

OTHER ROCKIN' ROSE SONGS

Rose Garden   Lynne Anderson
Rose Darling   Steely Dan
Ramble On Rose   Grateful Dead
It Must Have Been the Roses   Grateful Dead
Infrared Roses   Grateful Dead
Yankee Rose   David Lee Roth
Rosie Had Everything Planned   Supertramp
My Sister Rose   10,000 Maniacs
Spanish Rose   Santana
Kiss From a Rose   Seal
Rose Coloured Glasses   Raspberries
Spanish Rose   Van Morrison
Ro Ro Rosey   Van Morrison
Roses Blue   Joni Mitchell
For the Roses   Joni Mitchell
Whole Lotta Rosie   AC/DC
Rosie   Joan Armatrading
Black Rose   John Cale
Summer Roses   Willie Nelson
Really Rosie   Carole King

Rosemary
Smile a Little Smile for Me   Flying Machine

A sweet-sad tune by the one-hit group Flying Machine.

Smile songs are always good for a baby (*see* Sarah), because not only do babies smile easily, they also bawl their brains out at the drop of a hat. So *Smile a Little Smile* will work for you if your Rosemary is colicky, or has a blue streak, or is merely fussy, or cries at all. (Needless to say, this song should work for *every* Rosemary.)

OTHER ROCKIN' ROSEMARY SONGS

Rosemary   Randy Newman
Love Grows (Where My   Edison Lighthouse
Rosemary Goes)
Lily, Rosemary, and the Jack of Hearts   Bob Dylan
Rosemary   Grateful Dead
Rosemary's Wine   Neil Diamond

Rosetta
Rosetta   Willie Nelson

Roxanne
Roxanne   Police

No need to dwell on the subject matter here—a red-light Roxanne whom the singer is trying to coax into retirement. It doesn't really matter: what's crucial about this song is that people are going to follow your daughter around all of her life belting, "ROX-anne!" And even if it were Sting's voice, that could still get old.

So, if you're okay with this, and you think your girl will be, go for it.

Roy
Roy Rogers   Elton John
Hats Off to Roy Harper   Led Zeppelin
Fifty Ways to Leave Your Lover   Paul Simon

Ruby
Ruby Tuesday   Rolling Stones

This song works as a name song on so many levels it seems to have been written as one. Let's face it, your baby's going to "change with every new day." So yes, you can "hang a name" on her.

OTHER ROCKIN' RUBY SONGS

Ruby, Don't Take Your Love to Town	Kenny Rogers and First Edition
Ruby Baby	Dion
Ruby Dear	Talking Heads

Rudy
Rudy   Supertramp

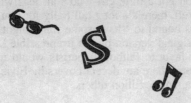

Sadie

Sexie Sadie   Beatles

A rather harsh song for a baby, but maybe you've got one who you think is destined to deceive, to promise more than she can deliver—like the song's Sadie.

Trivia: This song was actually about the Beatles' relationship with the Maharishi Mahesh Yogi and his Transcendental Meditation movement, with which the Beatles were briefly but enthusiastically involved in the late sixties. The Fab Four decided he was a false prophet, and the song was a thinly veiled exposé of him.

OTHER ROCKIN' SADIE SONGS

In Search of Little Sadie   Bob Dylan
Sadie   Spinners
Miss Sadie Mae   John Lee Hooker

Sally

Long Tall Sally   Little Richard

Oh, *baby!* Another gem of an infant-rocker, a classic that's impossible to resist. This was the music that scared the daylights out of the grownups of the day: a song that kids just couldn't *not* dance to.

Have you got a little girl who's all legs when you hold her up? Well, there's a long tall Sally for you. And a little one who is bound to "have some fun tonight." Whew!

If the original version by the irrepressible Little Richard isn't your favorite (although purists would argue it's the *only* version), there are decent covers by Elvis, the Beatles, Sha Na Na, and a zillion others.

OTHER ROCKIN' SALLY SONGS

Sally Can't Dance   Lou Reed
Lay Down Sally   Eric Clapton
Sally Go 'Round the Roses   Jaynettes
Mustang Sally   Commitments (originally
Wilson Pickett)
Sally   Sade
Sally Sue Brown   Bob Dylan
Sally Simpson   Who
Be My Girl—Sally   Police
Sally   Paul McCartney and Wings
Sally Mae   John Lee Hooker
Mustang Sally and GTO   John Lee Hooker

Samantha
Lady Samantha   Elton John

Samson
Samson and Delilah   Grateful Dead

Samuel
Don't Step on the Grass, Sam   Steppenwolf

This is a highly specialized type of song—but then you may be a parent with highly specialized interests. If you're one of those suburban homeowners, like Hank Hill of "King of the Hill," who spends more time tending to your lawn than planning your retirement—if you have actually gone to the trouble to enter "Best Lawn" contests—well, then you're going to need an anthem that instills in your little one the importance of keeping up the health and appearance of your outdoor carpet.

So name your boy Sam, and you'll always be able to tell him, "Don't step on the grass."

OTHER ROCKIN' SAM SONGS

Small Sad Sam   Phil McLean
Lucifer Sam   Pink Floyd
Muddy, Sam, and Otis   Rod Stewart

Sandy

4th of July, Asbury Park (Sandy)   Bruce Springsteen
Sandy   Dion

Sarah

Sara Smile   Daryl Hall and John Oates

Grown men—unselfconscious dads—have been known to sing this song in public to their little Sarahs, trying to coax a grin out of their little girls. And why not? The Hall and Oates ballad is pretty and sincere, and as good a smile-coaxer as there is on the market.

OTHER ROCKIN' SARAH SONGS

Sara   Starship
Sara   Fleetwood Mac
Sarah Maria   James Taylor
Me and Sarah Jane   Genesis
Sara   Bob Dylan
Sarah Maria   James Taylor

Scarlet
Scarlet   U2

Seamus
Seamus   Pink Floyd

Shandi
Shandi   Kiss

Shannon
Shannon   Henry Gross

This lugubrious ballad, the only solo hit by Henry Gross (who performed at Woodstock as a member of Sha Na Na), is all the more doleful when one realizes it's about a dog (that would be Shannon) who went swimming without a lifeguard one day, with tragic results.

As such, it doesn't seem like much of a baby-name song. But who knows? Maybe you've got a baby whose life is a dog. And it could be a useful teaser for your little girl when she's a headstrong terrible-two and wanders into, say, the basement against your instructions. A quick chorus of *Shannon* should bring her back.

Trivia: This song resembles a Beach Boys ballad more than a little, and there was a connection: it was based on a real Shannon, a dog owned by Gross's friend, Beach Boy Carl Wilson, that met a similar fate.

Sharona
My Sharona   Knack

It may be that you want to evoke the spirit of the seventies in your baby, that you want a hoppin', funky, fun-lovin' little girl. If so, the name for you may be Sharona, a name immortalized in the classic 1976 song (and also featured to great effect in the film *Reality Bites*).

Sheena
Sheena is a Punk Rocker   Ramones

You may have cut your teeth on nice music by nice artists like John Denver and Neil Diamond, music that your parents never minded hearing played in the house. Yup, you were a good kid. Well, this is almost a guarantee that your daughter, to your horror, will crank the Clash and the Sex Pistols, tie-die her mohawk, staple her nose, and use your beloved Bee Gees records to cut pizzas.

What can you do? Not much. Name her Sheena, after the Ramones song, and just accept that she's a punk rocker.

Sheila

Oh, Sheila Ready for the World
Sheila Tommy Roe
Shela Aerosmith
Sheila, Take a Bow Smiths

Shelly

Some of Shelly's Blues Linda Ronstadt

Sherry

Sherry Four Seasons

Of all the famous falsetto songs, sung by famous falsetto performers like the Beach Boys or Del Shannon or Smokey Robinson or the Bee Gees, none is *more* falsetto than *Sherry*, the debut single of the Four Seasons. Lead singer Frankie Valli's vocal sounds like something a ten-year-old would come out with if he'd consumed way too much sugar.

Be careful with this one if you actually expect to sing it to your child. Recommended: vocals transposed into the male baritone range, or sung by females with tender voices. Singing this song to your Sherry-baby as it was recorded could damage her ears, not to mention your crystal.

OTHER ROCKIN' SHERRY SONGS

Oh, Sherrie Steve Perry
Sherry Darling Bruce Springsteen

Simon

Simon Smith and the Dancing Bear   Randy Newman
Simon   Joan Armatrading

Sloopy

Hang On Sloopy   The McCoys

Most children are born with awesome physical attributes such as incredible lungs that can wake the dead. Another impressive feature of most babies is their viselike grip. This grip serves them well as they learn to hold a bottle or furniture as they learn or walk, or—if shy—a Mommy's skirt.

For those times when the grip is less than perfect, you many need to encourage the little one to "hang on." Whether or not you want to name the child Sloopy is another matter.

Sonny

Sonny Think Twice   Chicago
Sonny   Rod Stewart

Stanley

Stanley's Song   Byrds
Mrs. Stanley's Garden   Four Seasons
Fifty Ways to Leave Your Lover   Paul Simon

Stella

Stella Blue   Grateful Dead
Stella Mae   John Lee Hooker

Stephen

St. Stephen   Grateful Dead

You may be blessed with one of those kids who is forever preoccupied with subjects that are fathoms deep and likes to speak in riddles. If so, then you've got a little St. Stephen on your hands. So name him after the Grateful Dead tune. It will keep the little bugger busy for a lifetime just trying to figure out the lyrics.

Stephanie
Stephanie Says　　Velvet Underground

Stuart
Boogie with Stu　　Led Zeppelin

There are plenty of songs for a little dancing baby, and some, like this one, are for those who like a little edge to their boogying. ("Rock, rock, rock!")

So if you're a Zeppelin freak and have a baby who's born to boogie, name him Stu, and you'll always have a tune for boogying with him.

Sunny
When Sunny Gets Blue　　Kenny Rankin

Everybody has their off days. Even children go through periods where they may not feel like themselves. In such moments you can sing this pretty and consoling number to your child. (If you have a pretty voice like Kenny Rankin, all the better.)

Susan

Wake Up, Little Susie   Everly Brothers

This is a great song if you prefer a reverie to a lullaby. Never mind that waking up in this song is about a couple who stayed out too long.

It's an all-purpose wake-up call: You can sing this song to your Susie when she's an infant and has napped long enough, or when she's a toddler and is waking up at a snail's pace, or when she's a teenager dozing off during one of your long lectures.

The Everly Brothers version is the original and the classic, but you Deadheads know all too well that there are many versions of this song recorded by the Grateful Dead— it was a concert favorite.

> *Groovy Little Suzy*   Little Richard
> *Suzy Hang Around*   ABBA
> *Oh No Not Susan*   Electric Light Orchestra
> *Susie and Jeffrey*   Blondie
> *Susie*   John Lee Hooker

Susannah

Oh, Susannah   Byrds, James Taylor

Even if you haven't come from Alabama with a banjo on your knee, you may be a fan of American folk standards like *Oh, Susannah*. And since artists like James Taylor and the Byrds recorded it, it even sneaks into the rock catalog.

It's useful, too. Since many babies, when they're not crawlin', are bawlin', you'll be glad to have a song that coaxes them away from their tears.

ANOTHER ROCKIN' SUSANNAH SONG

Susannah's Still Alive   Kinks

Suzanne
Suzanne   Randy Newman
Suzanne   Neil Diamond
Suzanne   Journey

Sylvia
Sylvia's Mother   Dr. Hook and Medicine Show
Sylvia   Elvis Presley
Sylvia   Stevie Wonder

Tara
Tara   Roxy Music

Thelonius
Thelonius   Jeff Beck

Theodore/Teddy
Teddy Bear (Let Me Be Your)   Elvis Presley

Now, usually one gives a teddy bear to a child, and it's the bear that's named Teddy. Still, there's a lot to be said for a child that's so cuddly and cute that you think of him as *your* teddy bear.

Plus it's probably the most famous song by Elvis with a name in the title, so if you want a name that honors The King, go for it.

OTHER ROCKIN' TEDDY SONGS

Ready Teddy   Little Richard
Teddy Boy   Paul McCartney and Wings

Thomas
Tommy Can You Hear Me   Who

For Who buffs who want to name their child in honor of the enduring rock opera debuted at Woodstock, Tommy is a great name.

It's a useful name too. In your child's infancy, you can test his auditory response by singing him this tune.

OTHER ROCKIN' THOMAS SONGS

Tom's Diner	Suzanne Vega
The Only Living Boy in New York	Simon and Garfunkel
Major Tom	Peter Schilling
Pool Tom	Led Zeppelin
Ghost of Tom Joad	Bruce Springsteen
Tom Sawyer	Rush
Tom Traubert's Blues (Waltzing Matilda)	Rod Stewart
Space Oddity	David Bowie

Tracy

Tracy   Cufflinks
Christopher Tracy's Song   Prince

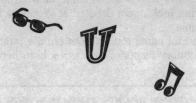

Ulysses
Tales of Brave Ulysses   Cream

Valerie
Valerie   Steve Winwood

Your daughter may feign great independence at times, acting like she never needs help of any kind—especially from her parents. Nonetheless, as the wise parent, you know full well that she's essentially helpless until she's a big kid (thirty or so).

Ever wise and patient, you can calmly assure your daughter that she can always "call on you." Which makes Valerie a good name for her.

OTHER ROCKIN' VALERIE SONGS

Valleri   Monkees
Valarie   Zappa/Mothers

Venus
Venus   Bananarama

Your daughter may be more than merely the most precious child in the world. She may be—and fortunately you have complete objectivity here—a *major talent*.

Never mind that many parents think their child has star potential—your baby, "she's got it."

In which case, she's your Venus.

111

Vera
Vera   Pink Floyd
Revenge of Vera Gemini   Blue Oyster Cult

Veronica
Veronica   Elvis Costello

This big hit by Elvis Costello has dense lyrics that'll never have anything to do with your little girl. Still, the catchy chorus offers a great peek-a-boo game for when your little girl decides she can hide away just by putting her hands over her face.

When she's older, boys may try to impress her by reeling off all the verses of this song. But, like the song's Veronica, she'll just laugh at them.

Victoria
Victoria   Kinks

Vincent
Vincent   Don McLean

Viola
Viola Lee Blues   Grateful Dead

Violet
Ultra Violet (Light My Way)   U2

Your baby may be the light of your life. You may feel as though your little one is the brightest bulb in your world. If so, name your little ray of sunshine Violet, as in Ultra Violet, and let her light your way.

OTHER ROCKIN' VIOLET SONGS

Violet (Live a Little Love a Little)   Elvis Presley
Violet   Seal

Virgil
Me and Virgil   Genesis

Virginia
Leave Virginia Alone   Rod Stewart

You might have a daughter who is a little eccentric and likes to spend time alone. If so, you might name her Virginia and use this Rod Stewart song to encourage the other kids to leave her alone.

OTHER ROCKIN' VIRGINIA SONGS

Sweet Virginia   Rolling Stones
West Virginia Fantasies   Chicago

Walter

Walter's Walk   Led Zeppelin
Walter's Blues   Rush

Warren

You're So Vain   Carly Simon

Now, the name Warren doesn't appear in the title or lyrics to this song, so why is it here? Because—this song is about Warren Beatty. The young Ms. Simon apparently had a fling with the dashing film star, who was notorious until just recently for sowing his wild oats among young, rich, and famous females.

Anyway, Warren is a nice enough name, but you may want to think twice about it as a baby name. If he were to turn out like the character in this song, he'd be one to laze away days at the track and chase solar eclipses. He could even end up in a film with Madonna. Yikes.

Wendell

Wendell Gee   R.E.M.

Wendy

Wendy   Beach Boys

The Beach Boys' manic classic reminds us that even the sweetest of girls can break boy's hearts. If you think you've got a little heartbreaker on your hands (and most parents do), Wendy may be the name.

Dads, be careful if you think you're actually going to

sing this song to your daughter. You may think your falsetto is as sweet as the Beach Boys' Brian Wilson, but more likely you sound like Adam Sandler. Would you want Opera Man singing to your little girl?

Trivia: Wendy Wilson of Wilson Phillips, whose dad Brian wrote *Wendy*, has a real-life rockin' baby name—her parents named her for the Beach Boys song.

OTHER ROCKIN' WENDY SONGS

Windy	Association
Born to Run	Bruce Springsteen
Wendy Time	Cure

Wesley
John Wesley Harding   Bob Dylan

William/Billy
Don't Lose My Number   Phil Collins

If you think you have an absent-minded kid, and you need a name for boy and not a girl (*see* Rikki), then, well, you're in luck. This Phil Collins song is made to order.

Kids lose all kinds of numbers—phone numbers, addresses, social security numbers . . . Yup, this is a practical song.

OTHER ROCKIN' WILLIAM SONGS

Wedding Bell Blues	Fifth Dimension (originally Laura Nyro)
Billy, Don't Be A Hero	Bo Donaldson and The Heywoods (originally Paper Lace)
My Girl Bill	Jim Stafford
Don't Mess With Bill	Marvelettes

Little Willy   Sweet
Willie and the Hand Jive   Johnny Otis Show
The Continuing Story of Bungalow Bill   Beatles
Billy Bones and the White Bird   Elton John
Wild Billy's Circus Story   Bruce Springsteen
Billy the Mountain   Zappa/Mothers
Little Billy   Who
The Ballad of Billy the Kid   Billy Joel
Blind Wille McTell   Bob Dylan
Pat Garrett & Billy the Kid   Bob Dylan
Billy   Bob Dylan
Billy 4   Bob Dylan
Billy 7   Bob Dylan
Little Billy   Who
Bill   Talking Heads
William, It Was Really Nothing   Smiths
Free Will   Rush
Will Gaines   Rush
Willy   Joni Mitchell
Crazy Captain Gunboat Willie   Little Feat
Country Willie   Willie Nelson
Ferryboat Bill   Velvet Underground

Woody

Song to Woody   Bob Dylan
Woody and Dutch on the Slow Train   Rickie Lee Jones

Yoko
The Ballad of John and Yoko   Beatles

Long before *Stop Pressuring Me*, John Lennon used this song to ask the world to please cut him a little slack. And he immortalized the name of his new wife—although in time she surely would have pulled that off on her own.

Well, perhaps you're a big Lennon fan, maybe even a big Ono fan. If you *must* name your child Yoko, go for it. Think twice, though: such a name might get your kid beat up on the playground. Plus, you will have handed your child an all-purpose excuse for misbehaving. Whenever she acts up and you demand an explanation, she'll shrug and say, "Christ, you *know* it ain't easy!" And the joke will be on you.

OTHER ROCKIN' YOKO SONGS

Dear Yoko   John Lennon
Oh Yoko!   John Lennon

Yvette
Yvette in English   Joni Mitchell

Zacchary
Zacchary and Jennifer   John Denver

Part 2
BY GROUP

You may be one of those Grateful Dead fans who's been to hundreds of concerts, with a meticulous scrapbook of all the playlists. And now you're looking for the perfect name for your baby—one you can be grateful for.

On the other hand, you may not be a rabid fan of any group. But, secretly, quietly, you've always thought that, say, the Spinners were the coolest thing. (There *are* such folks.)

That's what this section of *Rock 'n' Roll Baby Names* is all about. Regardless of who your favorite group is, or why you might want to immortalize them, you can find a baby name for more than 150 groups and artists, past and present, in the following pages.

Some names are sweet, some are mean, some have in-jokes associated with them—and some have virtually nothing to do with the group.

The names of the band members are also provided. You never know, you may not realize the perfect name for you baby until you see a group member's name. ("Pigpen—that's it!")

ABBA

Rumor had it that this Swedish double date couldn't even speak English, but simply pronounced the words. That turned out to be false. Not only was their English pretty good, but they contributed a list of songs you can use to name a baby, if you're so inclined.

Mama Mia could work well—your child's first words could have your name *and* hers.

The Songs

Angel	*Angel Eyes*
Bobby	*Me and Bobby and Bobby's Brother*
Chiquita	*Chiquita*
Fernando	*Fernando*
Helen	*Hey Hey Helen*
Mia	*Mama Mia*
Suzy	*Suzy Hang Around*

The Group

Agnetha	Agnetha Faltskog
Anni-Frid	Anni-Frid Lyngstad
Benny	Benny Andersson
Bjorn	Bjorn Ulvaeus

AC/DC

Most pediatricians probably wouldn't recommend too many volts of this group, but if you feel like you have a baby with a lot of current flowing through him or her, here are a few songs to choose from.

The Songs

Bonny	*Bonny*
Jack	*Jack*
Nick	*Nick of Time*
Rosie	*Whole Lotta Rosie*

The Group

Angus	Angus Young
Brian	Brian Johnson
Cliff	Cliff Williams
Malcolm	Malcolm Young
Phil	Phil Rudd

Aerosmith

This group has managed to successfully reinvent itself for the nineties, even though its members are old enough to be rockin' granddads.

No matter. If skinny fifty-year-old hard rockers turn you on, here's a slew of names for you.

The Songs

Adam	*Adam's Apple*
Angel	*Angel*
Barbara	*Major Barbara*
Chiquita	*Chiquita*
Janie	*Janie's Got A Gun*
Joanie	*Joanie's Butterfly*
	Prelude to Joanie
John	*St. John*
Mia	*Mia*
Pandora	*Pandora's Box*
Shela	*Shela*
Simoriah	*Simoriah*

The Group

Brad	Brad Whitford
Joe	Joe Perry
Joey	Joey Kramer
Steven	Steven Tyler
Tom	Tom Hamilton

Alice Cooper

This Alice is a man who once posed with his own baby in dramatic glitter-rock makeup. So don't let anyone ever tell you this is not a wholesome family man!

Not many baby names to choose from, but the man himself inspires one of the great unisex names of the rock era: Alice!

The Songs

Alma	*Alma Mater*
Dwight	*Ballad of Dwight Fry*
Ethyl	*Cold Ethyl*

Allman Brothers

The seminal southern rock group offers no shortage of baby names. Many are classics, many are instrumentals, most are girls' names. You may have a sweet Melissa, or a little Martha, or a pretty Jessica.

For boys' names you may want to go to the group itself. Keep in mind, though, that too many of the band members had bad luck with motorcycles.

The Songs

Elizabeth	*In Memory of Elizabeth Reed*
Jessica	*Jessica*
John	*Louisiana Lou and 3-Card Monty John*
Lou	*Louisiana Lou and 3-Card Monty John*
Martha	*Martha*
Melissa	*Melissa*
Monty	*Louisiana Lou and 3-Card Monty John*

The Group

Berry	Berry Oakley
Butch	Butch Trucks
Dick	Dick Betts
Duane	Duane Allman
Gregg	Gregg Allman
Jai	Jai Johanny Johanson

Joan Armatrading

If you have triplets—two girls and a boy—you can name them Rosie, Simon, and Joan, and exhaust the baby name possibilities of this artist.

The Songs

Rosie	*Rosie*
Simon	*Simon*

Atlanta Rhythm Section

The Songs

Angel	*Angel (What in the World's Come Over Us)*
Dora	*Doraville*
Evelyn	*Evilene*
Georgia	*Georgia Rhythm*
Lois	*Ballad of Lois Malone*
Quinella	*Quinella*

The Group

Barry	Barry Bailey
Dean	Dean Daughtry
J. R.	J. R. Cobb
Paul	Paul Goddard
Robert	Robert Nix
Ronnie	Ronnie Hammond

The Band

This group, which always looked as if it had been photographed during the Civil War, offers plenty of baby name songs.

There's also *Get up Jake*, a beauty if you have a son destined to be a night-person who you'll need to get out of bed at, say, two in the afternoon.

The Songs

Annie	*The Weight*
Bessie	*Bessie Smith*
Daniel	*Daniel and The Sacred Harp*
Dixie	*The Night They Drove Old Dixie Down*
Evangeline	*Evangeline*
Henry	*Don't Ya Tell Henry*
Jake	*Get Up Jake*
Jericho	*Caves of Jericho*
Katie	*Katie's Been Gone*
Ophelia	*Ophelia*

The Group

Garth	Garth Hudson
Levon	Levon Helm
Richard	Richard Manuel
Rick	Rick Danko
Robbie	Robbie Robertson

Bangles

Not a lot of songs to choose from, but there's always the Bangle names themselves.

So, if this is your group, and you have a little girl-group kind of girl, go for Debbi, Susanna, or Vicki.

The Songs

Angel	*Angels Don't Fall in Love*
James	*James*

The Group

Debbi	Debbi Peterson
Michael	Michael Steele
Susanna	Susanna Hoffs
Vicki	Vicki Peterson

Beach Boys

Fans of the kings of surf will find plenty of songs to immortalize an offspring (*see* Wendy, Rhonda). Some are pretty quirky: songs about street hot rods (*Ballad of Ole Betsy*), Santa's hot rod (*Little Saint Nick*), and talk show hosts (*Johnny Carson*).

More mainstream, and better for a baby name, is *Barbara Ann*. The Boys' cover of the earlier Regents hit was recorded "studio live," complete with background patter, giggles, and off-key singing, which, of course, makes it a perfect singalong for the average pitchfork-free singer. So take your little girl's hand and start her rockin' and a-rollin'. And a-reelin' too.

Beach Boys (cont'd)

The Songs

Angel	*Angel Come Home*
Anna Lee	*Anna Lee, the Healer*
Barbara Ann	*Barbara Ann*
Betsy	*Ballad of Ole Betsy*
Carl	*Carl's Big Chance*
Caroline	*Caroline No*
Deirdre	*Deirdre*
Denny	*Denny's Drums*
Diane	*My Diane*
John	*Sloop John B*
	Johnny Carson
	Johnny B. Goode
Judy	*Judy*
Lana	*Lana*
Louie	*Louie Louie*
Lynda	*Lady Lynda*
Marcella	*Marcella*
Mona	*Mona*
Nick	*Little Saint Nick*
Peggy Sue	*Peggy Sue*
Rhonda (Ronda)	*Help Me, Rhonda / Ronda*
Susie	*Susie Cincinnati*
Wendy	*Wendy*

The Group

Alan	Alan Jardine
Brian	Brian Wilson
Bruce	Bruce Johnston
Carl	Carl Wilson
Dennis	Dennis Wilson
Mike	Mike Love

Beastie Boys

If you've given birth to a little beastie boy or beastie girl, there are some good songs to choose from here.

The Songs

Eugene	*Eugene's Lament*
Janice	*Ask for Janice*
Jimi	*Jimi*
James / Jimmy	*Jimmy James*
Johnny	*Johnny Ryall*
Michelle	*Michelle's Farm*
Paul	*Paul Revere*
Ricky	*Ricky's Lament*
Sabrosa	*Sabrosa*

The Group

Adam	Adam Horovitz
	Adam Yauch
Adrock	Adam Horovitz
MCA	Adam Yauch
Michael	Michael Diamond

Beatles

For the millions of Beatles fans, there seem to be almost as many baby name songs sung by the Fab Four.

There are baby names for all kinds of babies, be they dear (Prudence), dizzy (Lizzie), long and tall (Sally), lovely (Rita), or even sexy (Sadie). Boy names are less common, but still weigh in with Bill, John, Robert, Maxwell, and Rocky. There are even songs immortalizing Yoko and Ringo, if you insist. "Yeah, yeah, *yeah!*"

The Songs

Anna	*Anna (Go to Him)*
Bill	*The Continuing Story of Bungalow Bill*
Eleanor	*Eleanor Rigby*
John	*Ballad of John and Yoko*
Jude	*Hey Jude*
Julia	*Julia*
Lizzie	*Dizzie Miss Lizzie*
Lucy	*Lucy in the Sky with Diamonds*
Madonna	*Lady Madonna*
Maggie	*Maggie May*
Martha	*Martha My Dear*
Maxwell	*Maxwell's Silver Hammer*
Michelle	*Michelle*
Pam	*Polythene Pam*
Penny	*Penny Lane*
Prudence	*Dear Prudence*
Ringo	*Ringo* (by Lorne Greene)
Rita	*Lovely Rita*
Robert	*Doctor Robert*
Rocky	*Rocky Raccoon*
Sadie	*Sexy Sadie*
Sally	*Long Tall Sally*
Yoko	*Ballad of John and Yoko*

The Group

George   George Harrison
John   John Lennon
Paul   Paul McCartney
Ringo   Ringo Starr

Jeff Beck

For you Jeff Beck fans (a few zillion of you), let's face it, the most logical name is after the man himself, Jeff—for *Jeff's Blues*, *Jeff's Boogie*, and Jeff Beck.

And if you have a girl, well, consider Jeff.

The Songs

Jeff   *Jeff's Boogie*
            Jeff's Blues
Jody   *Jody*
John   *Who Slapped John*
Thelonius *Thelonius*

131

Bee Gees

The only group in history whose voices got *higher* as they got older. (In a few years, only dogs will be able to hear them.)

If you want to name your child after this group, there are a few songs to choose from. None are terribly famous, though. So if you're lovin' your baby and this group inside out (whatever *that* means), you may want to name him or her after the brothers themselves.

The Songs

Angel	*Fallen Angel*
Elisa	*Elisa*
Fanny	*Fanny (Be Tender with My Love)*
Geoffrey	*Sir Geoffrey Saved the World*
Juliet	*In Concert: Juliet*

The Group

Barry	Barry Gibb
Maurice	Maurice Gibb
Robin	Robin Gibb

Chuck Berry

The granddaddy of guitar-flashin', duck-walkin' rock 'n' roll, Chuck Berry penned so many great songs, he could have his own baby-name book.

Take your pick of classics: Johnny B. Goode, Maybellene, Nadine, Little Marie . . .

For just about any song, chances are it's a classic and there are probably about five hundred versions of it available by groups from the Stones to the Beatles to the Grateful Dead.

The Songs

Anthony	*Anthony Boy*
Betty Jean	*Betty Jean*
Carol	*Carol*
Delilah	*Beautiful Delilah*
Jo Jo	*Jo Jo Gunne*
Johnny	*Bye Bye Johnny*
	Johnny B. Goode
Marie	*Little Marie*
Maybellene	*Maybellene*
Nadine	*Nadine (Is It You)*
Pedro	*Hey Pedro*
Ramona	*Ramona Says Yes*

Blind Faith

(*see* Eric Clapton, Steve Winwood)

Blondie

If you're fond of Deborah Harry's enormously successful group from the seventies and eighties, there aren't too many songs to choose from, especially famous ones.

Blondie (cont'd)

Still, you may just consider naming your child Blondie, especially if he or she is a little tow-head. Why not?

The Songs

Caesar	*Little Caesar*
Denis	*Denis*
Jeffrey	*Susie and Jeffrey*
Susie	*Susie and Jeffrey*

The Group

Chris	Chris Stein
Clem	Clem Burke
Deborah	Deborah Harry
Frank	Frank Infante
Jimmy	Jimmy Destri
Nigel	Nigel Harrison

Blue Oyster Cult

The Songs

Angel	*Fallen Angel*
Debbie	*Debbie Denise*
Denise	*Debbie Denise*
Joan	*Joan Crawford*
Vera	*Revenge of Vera Gemini*

The Group

Albert	Albert Bouchard
Allen	Allen Lanier
Buck	Donald "Buck Dharma" Roeser

Donald	Donald "Buck Dharma" Roeser
Eric	Eric Bloom
Joe	Joe Bouchard

David Bowie

There probably is a person or two walking around named Ziggy, and you can bet the parents spent the seventies visiting other galaxies while at Bowie concerts.

If that's a little too way-out for you, fortunately there's also a slew of more conventional names to choose from.

The Songs

Aladdin	*Alladin Sane*
Andy	*Andy Warhol*
Arthur	*Uncle Arthur*
Athena	*Pallas Athena*
Bob	*Song for Bob Dylan*
Emily	*See Emily Play*
Jane	*Liza Jane*
Jean	*Blue Jean*
	Jean Genie
Joe	*Joe the Lion*
John	*John, I'm Only Dancing*
Lester	*Looking for Lester*
Liza	*Liza Jane*
Louie	*Louie Louie Go Home*
Lucy	*Lucy Can't Dance*
Roslyn	*Roslyn*
Ziggy	*Ziggy Stardust*

Buffalo Springfield

Not a lot of songs in this influential group's catalog, and no candidates whatsoever if you're looking for a conventional girl's name. Still, there are the names of the group itself—for what they're worth.

The Songs

Clancy — *Nowadays Clancy Can't Even Sing*

The Group

Bruce	Bruce Palmer
Dewey	Dewey Martin
Doug	Doug Hastings
Jim	Jim Messina
Neil	Neil Young
Richie	Richie Furay
Stephen	Stephen Stills

Jimmy Buffett

The Songs

Caroline	*Woman Going Crazy on Caroline Street*
Dee	*Ellis Dee*
Ellis	*Ellis Dee*
Elvis	*Elvis Impersonators*
Frank	*Frank and Lola*

John	*Ballad of Spider John*
	Uncle John's
Lola	*Frank and Lola*
Morris	*Morris' Nightmare*
Salome	*When Salome Plays the Drum*

The Byrds

Byrds aficionados are passionate about their group, and this loyal core has kept the group's albums in print for decades.

And there are plenty of songs to choose from for naming your little boy or gyrl—particularly if he or she is pretty—like boy Floyd or Polly—which undoubtedly he or she is.

The Songs

Floyd	*Pretty Boy Floyd*
Joe	*Hey Joe*
John	*John Riley*
	Old John Robertson
Kathleen	*Kathleen's Song*
Mae	*Mae Jean Goes to Hollywood*
Polly	*Pretty Polly*
Stanley	*Stanley's Song*
Susannah	*Oh Susannah!*

The Group

Chris	Chris Hillman
Clarence	Clarence White
David	David Crosby
Gene	Gene Parsons
	Gene Clark
Gram	Gram Parsons
Jay	Jay York

The Byrds (cont'd)

The Group

Jim	Jim McGuinn
Michael	Michael Clarke
Roger	Roger McGuinn

B-52s

This cheeky, spacy group managed to fly close enough to Planet Earth to offer some perfectly fine songs for naming your baby.

Planet Claire is particularly fine if you see your child as some celestial wonder. (If you're a big fan of this group you may well see things that way.)

The Songs

Claire	*Planet Claire*
June	*Junebug*
Lorraine	*Quiche Lorraine*
Mo	*Is that You Mo-Dean?*
Venus	*53 Miles West of Venus*

The Group

Cindy	Cindy Wilson
Fred	Fred Schneider
Kate	Kate Pierson
Keith	Keith Strickland
Ricky	Ricky Wilson

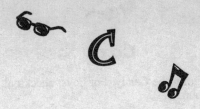

John Cale

(see also Velvet Underground)

The Songs

Adelaide	*Adelaide*
Casey	*Casey at the Bat*
Carmen	*Soul of Carmen Miranda*
Dixie	*Dixieland Dixie*
Harry	*King Harry*
Hedda	*Hedda Gabler*
Helen	*Helen of Troy*
Jack	*Jack the Ripper*
John	*John Milton*
Milton	*John Milton*
Rose	*Black Rose*

Cars

For girls, it's got to be Candy. For boys, check out the members of the group.

The Songs

Candy   *Candy-O*

The Group

Benjamin   Benjamin Orr
David   David Robinson
Elliot   Elliot Easton
Gregg   Gregg Hawkes
Ric   Ric Ocasek

Chicago

The Songs

Alma   *Alma Mater*
Donna   *Prima Donna*
Harry   *Harry Truman*
Jenny   *Jenny*
Richard   *Song for Richard and His Friends*
Sonny   *Sonny Think Twice*
Virginia   *West Virginia Fantasies*

The Group

Daniel   Daniel Seraphine
James   James Pankow

Lee	Lee Loughnane
Peter	Peter Cetera
Robert	Robert Lamm
Terry	Terry Kath
Walter	Walter Parazaider

Eric Clapton

(includes Cream, Derek/Dominos, Blind Faith, Yardbirds)

The great (and reluctant) guitar hero has been with more groups than the average groupie. No matter—the decades have produced a phenomenal catalog of famous songs that are associated with him, whether or not he was in a group at the time. *Layla*, originally by Derek and the Dominos, is his angst-ridden plea to Patti Harrison (wife of George), with whom he was smitten at the time—and managed to coax away from George.

Lay Down Sally may not seem right for a baby, but in a way, it is: when she's a preschooler and has had too much sugar, you'll be saying that to her *a lot*.

The Songs

Bernard	*Bernard Jenkins*
Layla	*Layla*
Lucy	*Watch Out for Lucy*
Mae	*Rita Mae*
Pearl	*Pearly Queen*
Rachel	*Little Rachel*
Rita	*Rita Mae*
Rose	*Black Rose*
Sally	*Lay Down Sally*
Signe	*Signe*

Eric Clapton (cont'd)

The Songs

Ulysses	*Tales of Brave Ulysses*
Willie	*Willie and the Hand Jive*

(A few of) The Groups

Cream

Eric	Eric Clapton
Ginger	Ginger Baker
Jack	Jack Bruce

Derek and The Dominos

Bobby	Bobby Whitlock
Carl	Carl Radle
Duane	Duane Allman
Eric	Eric Clapton
Jim	Jim Gordon

Blind Faith

Eric	Eric Clapton
Ginger	Ginger Baker
Rick	Rick Grech
Steve	Steve Winwood

The Yardbirds

Chris	Chris Dreja
Eric	Eric Clapton
Jeff	Jeff Beck
Jimmy	Jim McCarty
	Jimmy Page
Keith	Keith Relf
Paul	Paul "Sam" Samwell-Smith

Phil Collins

(includes Genesis)

The Songs

Billy	*Don't Lose My Number*
Jane	*Me and Sarah Jane*
Lorenzo	*Lorenzo*
Sarah	*Me and Sarah Jane*
Virgil	*Me and Virgil*

The Group

Peter	Peter Gabriel
Phil	Phil Collins

Elvis Costello

Once an angry young man (he's since mellowed), the latter-day Elvis offers plenty of tunes to immortalize your child.

The Songs

Alison	*Alison*
Angel	*Poor Little Angel*
Chelsea	*(I Don't Want to Go to) Chelsea*
Georgie	*Georgie and Her Rival*
Jack	*Jack of All Parades*
Luther	*Luther's Army*

Elvis Costello (cont'd)

The Songs

Napoleon	*Poor Napoleon*
Oliver	*Oliver's Army*
Veronica	*Veronica*

Cream

(*see* Eric Clapton)

Creedence Clearwater Revival

Any parent who's changed a diaper has seen a *Bad Moon Rising.* Of course, there's no baby name in that song, but there are in several other of CCR's finest. All girl names—Molly, Mary, Susie, and so on—so if you have a boy, you're going to have to name him after one of the group, or get another group.

The Songs

Lodi	*Lodi*
Mary	*Proud Mary*

Mary Lou	*Hello, Mary Lou (Goodbye Heart)*
Molina	*Molina*
Molly	*Good Golly Miss Molly*
Susie	*Susie Q*

The Group

Doug	David Clifford
John	John Fogerty
Stuart	Stuart Cook
Tom	Tom Fogerty

Crosby, Stills, and Nash (and Young)

In its prime, this group could never seem to stay together for more than five minutes. (When they included Neil Young, make that *one* minute.)

Nonetheless, they penned and recorded some all-time classics, such as a debut album that included David Crosby's *Guinnevere*, which is perfect if you have a little girl with green eyes.

Of course those eyes could be . . . blue! No problem, there's *Suite: Judy Blue Eyes* (pun on *Sweet* Judy Blue Eyes), Stephen Stills's anthem to his former girlfriend with memorable eyes, Judy Collins.

If baby has *brown* eyes, well, you're out of luck, at least with Crosby, Stills, and Nash.

The Songs

Guinnevere	*Guinnevere*
Johnny	*Johnny's Garden*
Judy	*Suite: Judy Blue Eyes*
Lee	*Lee Shore*
Susan	*Song for Susan*

Crosby, Stills, and Nash (and Young) (cont'd)

The Group

David	David Crosby
Graham	Graham Nash
Neil	Neil Young
Stephen	Stephen Stills

The Cure

The Songs

Charlotte	*Charlotte Sometimes*
Elise	*Letter to Elise*
Wendy	*Wendy Time*

The Group

Laurence	Laurence Tolhurst
Robert	Robert Smith
Simon	Simon Gallup

Deep Purple

The Songs

Anya	*Anya*
Jack	*Jack D'or*
Lucille	*Lucille*
Morris	*Mighty Morris Ten*

The Group

Ian	Ian Paice
	Ian Gillan
Jon	Jon Lord
Ritchie	Ritchie Blackmore
Roger	Roger Glover

Depeche Mode

Okay, there will be no jokes about *Depressed* Mode here—oops, too late.

This group, popular among dramatically emotional (usually *downwardly* so) college students, offers but a couple of baby name songs, and they are, one could say, the alpha and omega of names: Judas and Jesus. Perfect!

The Songs

Jesus	*Personal Jesus*
Judas	*Judas*

The Group

Alan	Alan Wilder
Andrew	Andrew Fletcher
David	David Gahan
Martin	Martin Gore

John Denver

Rock purists may wince at the inclusion of the late balladeer, who was always more polite than petulant, but rock record shops have always gladly stocked this Country Boy's discs, because they sell like hotcakes.

Annie's Song is a good (and famous) tune for an Annie. She may just be the girl of your senses.

The Songs

Angel	*Angels From Montgomery*
Annie	*Annie's Song*
	Annie's Other Song
Darcy	*Darcy Farrow*
Esmerelda	*Esmerelda*
Isabel	*Isabel*
Jennifer	*Zacchary and Jennifer*
Jesse	*Whispering Jesse*
Matthew	*Matthew*
Molly	*Molly*
Zacchary	*Zacchary and Jennifer*

Derek and the Dominos

(*see* Eric Clapton)

Devo

Are you not parents? You are Devo! If so, name your baby Beulah or Jimmy or any of the others.

The Songs

Beulah	*Beulah*
Jimmy	*Jimmy*
Jocko	*Jocko Homo*
Jonee	*Come Back Jonee*

Devo (cont'd)

The Group

Alan	Alan Myers
Bob	Bob Mothersbaugh
Bob	Bob Casale
Jerry	Jerry Casale
Mark	Mark Mothersbaugh

Neil Diamond

The raspy-voiced pop rocker, who sold enough records to keep all of China's feet tappin', came up with plenty of tunes to name your baby.

Most of the names are for girls, though, unless you want to name your boy Neil, or Lee, after the much-covered *Stagger Lee*.

The Songs

Angel	*Angel*
Caroline	*Sweet Caroline*
Chelsea	*Chelsea Morning*
Desiree	*Desiree*
Holly	*Holly Holy*
Juliet	*Juliet*
Laura	*I'll See You on the Radio (Laura)*
Lee	*Stagger Lee*
Missa	*Missa*
Rosemary	*Rosemary's Wine*
Rose/Rosie	*Cracklin' Rosie*
Suzanne	*Suzanne*

Bo Diddley

Boy or girl, if you want to name your child after the seminal r&b writer and crooner who influenced scores of groups (especially the Stones), the inevitable choice is, of course, Bo.

The Songs

Bo	*Bo's Bounce*
	Bo's Guitar
Jerome	*Bring it to Jerome*
Josephine	*Ride on Josephine*
Mona	*Mona*

Dion

Bronx born-and-bred Dion Dimucci is hardly on many radar screens any more, but he managed to pen and perform some fabulous songs for naming babies.

Perhaps the best is *Runaround Sue*, which, although about a girl who's running around is of the heart-breaking variety, can also apply to any other running your little Sue does: clunky terrible-two wandering, track-star sprinting, first-job messengering . . . You name it.

The Songs

Abraham	*Abraham, Martin, and John*
Bobby	*Abraham, Martin, and John*
Diane	*Little Diane*
John	*Abraham, Martin, and John*
Lee	*Stagger Lee*

Dion (cont'd)

The Songs

Martin	*Abraham, Martin, and John*
Sandy	*Sandy*
Sue	*Runaround Sue*

Dire Straits

If you have opposite-sex twins you may *feel* like you're in dire straits. If you're in love with this group, though, just name them Romeo and Juliet and at least you don't have to worry about *that*.

The Songs

Angel	*Angel of Mercy*
Elvis	*Calling Elvis*
Juliet	*Romeo and Juliet*
Romeo	*Romeo and Juliet*

The Group

Alan	Alan Clark
Hal	Hal Lindes
John	John Illsley
Mark	Mark Knopfler
Terry	Terry Williams

Doobie Brothers

There are plenty of songs to choose from here. (Keep in mind though, that you're naming your child after a band that named itself after the evil weed.) The titles alone of songs like *Larry the Logger Two-Step* and *Neal's Fandango* make them excellent name inspirations. If you have a girl, couldn't she be a *Sweet Maxine*?

The Songs

Larry	*Larry the Logger Two-Step*
Maxine	*Sweet Maxine*
Neal	*Neal's Fandango*
Paul	*Slippery St. Paul*
Ukiah	*Ukiah*

The Group

Bobby	Bobby Lakind
Chet	Chet McCracken
Cornelius	Cornelius Bumpus
Jeffrey	Jeffrey Porter
	Jeffrey "Skunk" Baxter
John	John "Little John" Hartman
	John McFee
Keith	Keith Knudsen
Michael	Michael Hossack
	Michael McDonald
Pat	Pat Simmons
Skunk	Jeffrey "Skunk" Baxter
Tiran	Tiran Porter
Tom	Tom Johnston
Willie	Willie Weeks

Doors

Perhaps your child can name himself or herself. Take the lead from *Hello, I Love You*. Introduce yourself to your child, express the enormous affection you feel, and then ask if he or she will share with you that all-important name.

Okay, granted that'll never work in a million years, so name your daughter Maggie or Gloria, and name your son after someone in the band.

The Songs

Gloria	*Gloria*
Maggie	*Maggie McGill*

The Group

Jim	Jim Morrison
John	John Densmore
Ray	Ray Manzarek
Robby	Robby Krieger

Duran Duran

Well, some groups seem to think that having songs with names in the titles is just *beneath* them. Hmmmph!

No matter. There are other ways to immortalize this group with the redundant name. For example, if you last name is Johnson, name your child John; if the last name is Matthews, name him Matthew.

You-you get-get the-the idea-idea.

The Songs

None!

The Group

Andy	Andy Taylor
John	John Taylor
Nick	Nick Rhodes
Roger	Roger Taylor
Simon	Simon Le Bon

Bob Dylan

If you're among the millions of fans of this rock original, you've got your share of songs to choose from. Keep in mind, too, that Bobby (born Robert Zimmerman) got his name from the poet Dylan Thomas.

The Songs

Albert	*Frankie and Albert*
Alberta	*Alberta #1*
	Alberta #2
Angel	*You Angel You*
	Precious Angel
Arthur	*Arthur McBride*
Angelina	*Angelina*
	Farewell Angelina
Bessie	*Bessie Smith*
Billy	*Billy (Billy 4, Billy 7)*
	Pat Garrett and Billy the Kid
Bruce	*Lenny Bruce*
Dary	*Who Killed Dary Moore*
Davy	*Black Jack Davy*
Delia	*Delia (traditional)*

Bob Dylan (cont'd)

The Songs

Frankie	*Frankie and Albert*
Hattie	*The Lonesome Death of Hattie Carroll*
Hazel	*Hazel*
Henry	*Love Henry (traditional)*
Hollis	*Ballad to Hollis Brown*
Homer	*Open the Door, Homer*
Jack	*Lily, Rosemary, and the Jack of Hearts*
	Black Jack Davy
	Jack-a-Roe (traditional)
Jane	*Queen Jane Approximately*
Jim	*Jim Jones*
Joe/Joey	*Diamond Joe*
	Joey
	Tequilla Joe
Johanna	*Visions of Johanna*
John	*John Brown*
	John Wesley Harding
Katie	*Katie's Been Gone*
Lenny	*Lenny Bruce*
Lily	*Lily, Rosemary, and the Jack of Hearts*
Maggie	*Little Maggie*
	Maggie's Farm
Marie	*Absolutely Sweet Marie*
Mary	*Take a Message to Mary*
Pat	*Pat Garrett and Billy the Kid*
Peggy	*Peggy Day*
	Pretty Peggy-O
Percy	*Percy's Song*
Ramona	*To Ramona*
Rosemary	*Lily, Rosemary, and the Jack of Hearts*
Sadie	*In Search of Little Sadie*
Sally	*Sally Sue Brown*
Sara	*Sara*
Sue	*Sally Sue Brown*
Suze	*Suze (the Cough Song)*
Willie	*Blind Willie McTell*
Woody	*Song to Woody*

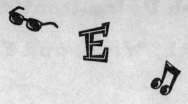

Eagles

Not much in the way of choice for girls, though you could consider Glenn, *a la* Glenn Close. For boys, your pickins are a bit better, but let's face it, the group that took it to the limit far *under*-exceeded its quota of name songs.

The Songs

| Dean | *James Dean* |
| James | *James Dean* |

The Group

Bernie	Bernie Leadon
Don	Don Henley
Glenn	Glenn Frey
Randy	Randy Meisner

Earth, Wind, and Fire

The Songs

Faith   *Interlude: Faith*

The Group

Alex	Alex Thomas
Chester	Chester Washington
Don	Don Whitehead
Leslie	Leslie Drayton
Maurice	Maurice White
Michael	Michael Beal
Phillard	Phillard Williams
Sherry	Sherry Scott
Verdine	Verdine White
Wade	Wade Flemons

Electric Light Orchestra

Name your boys after the group; for a girl—your little *Evil Woman*—you have some songs to work with.

Kajuma could be fun. Imagine this coming out of your mouth: "Put on your pajamas, Kajuma!" (Your child will grow up either amused or *unbelievably* angry.)

The Songs

Kajuma	*Kajuma*
Nellie	*Nellie Takes Her Bow*
Susan	*Oh No Not Susan*

The Group

Bev	Bev Bevan
Jeff	Jeff Lynne
Hugh	Hugh McDowall
Kelly	Kelly Groucutt
Melvyn	Melvyn Gale
Michael	Michael De Albuquerque
	Michael Edwards
Mik	Mik Kaminski
Richard	Richard Tandy

Emerson, Lake, and Palmer

Not the best group if you have a girl, although Juliet is a possibility.

If you have a boy, your little Lucky Man may be the type to pretend his bed is a trampoline. In such a case, you have a Benny (the Bouncer). And who knows, he may grow up to be someone who throws people out of bars.

The Songs

Abaddon	*Abaddon's Bolero*
Benny	*Benny the Bouncer*
Bo	*Bo Diddley*
Juliet	*Romeo and Juliet*
Peter	*Peter Gunn*
Romeo	*Romeo and Juliet*

The Group

Carl	Carl Palmer
Greg	Greg Lake
Keith	Keith Emerson

Brian Eno

The Songs

Ali	*Ali Click*
Cindy	*Cindy Tells Me*
Jezebel	*Jezebel Spirit*
Judy	*Back in Judy's Jungle*
Julie	*Julie*
Kurt	*Kurt's Rejoinder*
Pearl	*Pearl*
Pierre	*Pierre in Mist*

Erasure

The Songs

Gloria	*Gloria*

The Group

Andy	Andy Bell
Vince	Vince Clarke

Eurythmics

The Songs

Adrian	*Adrian*
Angel	*Angel*
Belinda	*Belinda*
Jennifer	*Jennifer*

The Group

Annie	Annie Lennox
David	David A. Stewart

Fleetwood Mac

The group that was taking off big-time just as it was falling apart offers many names.

The most famous is probably Rhiannon. Be advised, though, that this song was written for Stevie Nicks's, uh, *girl*friend. Just thought you'd want to know.

The Songs

Angel	*Angel*
Buddy	*Buddy's Song*
Caroline	*Caroline*
Crystal	*Crystal*
Danny	*Danny's Chant*
Diane	*Oh Diane*
Earl	*Earl Gray*
Jack	*Black Jack Blues*
Judy	*Jewel Eyed Judy*
Rhiannon	*Rhiannon*

The Groups (various)

Bob	Bob Welch
Christine	Christine McVie
Danny	Danny Kirwin
Jeremy	Jeremy Spencer
John	John McVie
Lindsey	Lindsey Buckingham

Mick	Mick Fleetwood
Peter	Peter Green
Stevie	Stevie Nicks

Four Seasons

For boys, use the group names. For girls, there are plenty to choose from for your baby—she might just be a Sherry baby.

The usual Falsetto Warning is in effect for this group: Dads, use extreme caution singing any of these songs to your child. You could hurt yourself *and* the child.

The Songs

Carol	*Carol of the Bells*
Connie	*Connie-O*
Dawn	*Dawn (Go Away)*
Emily	*Emily's*
Joy	*Joy to the World*
Marlene	*Marlena*
Ronnie	*Ronnie*
Sherry	*Sherry*
Stanley	*Mrs. Stanley's Garden*

The Group

Bob	Bob Gaudio
Frankie	Frankie Valli
Joe	Joe Long
Nick	Nick Massi
Tommy	Tommy De Vito

Peter Gabriel

(*see* Phil Collins)

J. Geils Band

The Songs

Angel   *Angel in Blue*

The Group

Danny   Danny Klein
J.   J. Geils
Magic   Magic Dick
Peter   Peter Wolf
Seth   Seth Justman
Stephen   Stephen Jo Bladd

Genesis

(*see* Phil Collins)

Go-Gos

All right, let's face it, the one boy name you can squeeze out of this group is probably totally unacceptable!

But there's still hope. If you're so gung-ho on naming your boy after this group (God only knows why you'd name a boy after a girl group), you can fiddle with the title a little: *Johnny, Aren't You Dear?* There, that's better.

The Songs

| Johnny | *Johnny, Are You Queer?* |

The Group

Belinda	Belinda Carlisle
Charlotte	Charlotte Caffey
Gina	Gina Schock
Jane	Jane Wiedlin
Kathy	Kathy Valentine
Margot	Margot Olivarria

Grateful Dead

It's chilling to think of naming a baby after some of these, which are either willfully zonked-out (*Rosemary*) or require, like *St. Stephen*, mind alteration for full comprehension (*not* recommended).

Nonetheless, despite all the scary imagery that goes with the Dead territory (no group has made better use of skeletons on their album covers), there are some great baby-name candidates here. The title *Little Nemo in Nightland* alone is good cause for having a little Nemo.

Remember, whatever you name your child, and whether it's a girl or boy, for a certain period it will be a Pigpen. Get used to it.

The Songs

Althea	*Althea*
Ann Marie	*Friend of the Devil*
Bertha	*Bertha*
Bobby	*Me and Bobby McGee*
Casey	*Casey Jones*
Cassidy	*Cassidy*
Charlie	*Cosmic Charlie*
	Mr. Charlie
Delilah	*Samson and Delilah*
Esau	*My Brother Esau*
Franklin	*Franklin's Tower*
Jack	*Jack Straw*
	Jack-a-Roe
Jed	*Tennessee Jed*
Jimmy	*Row Jimmy*
John/Johnny	*Uncle John's Band*
	Johnny B. Goode
Katie Mae	*Katie Mae*
Lee	*Stagger Lee*
Lucy	*Loose Lucy*
⸺mo	*Little Nemo in Nightland*

Peter	*Black Peter*
Rosalie	*Rosalie McFall*
Rose	*Ramble On Rose*
	It Must Have Been the Roses
	Infrared Roses
Rosemary	*Rosemary*
Samson	*Samson and Delilah*
Stella	*Stella Blue*
Stephen	*St. Stephen*
Susie	*Wake Up, Little Susie*
Viola	*Viola Lee Blues*

The Group

Bill	Bill Kreutzmann
Bob (Bobby)	Bob Weir
Donna	Donna Godchaux
Jerry	Jerry Garcia
Keith	Keith Godchaux
Mickey	Mickey Hart
Phil	Phil Lesh
Pigpen	Rod McKernan
Robert	Robert Hunter
Rod	Rod McKernan

Al Green

The Songs

Georgia	*Georgia Boy*
Grace	*Amazing Grace*
Judy	*Judy*

Guns 'n' Roses

For boys, go with the group. For girls, you sole choice is *My Michelle*.

The Songs

Michelle   *My Michelle*

The Group

Axl	W. Axl Rose
Duff	Duff "Rose" McKagen
Izzy	Izzy Stradlin'
Rose	Duff "Rose" McKagen
Slash	Slash
Steven	Steven Adler

Hall and Oates

A lot of snappy and pretty songs here.

If you have a girl, you won't be the first to be seen in public trying to coax a pleasing expression out of your daughter by holding her up and singing *Sara Smile*. Go for it.

The Songs

Georgie	*Georgie*
Kerry	*Kerry*
Lilly	*Lilly (Are You Happy?)*
Sara	*Sara Smile*

The Group

Daryl	Daryl Hall
John	John Oates

George Harrison

The Songs

Frankie	*Ballad of Sir Frankie Crisp*
Jack	*Jumpin' Jack Flash*
Johnny	*It's Johnny's Birthday*

Jimi Hendrix

Hendrix wasn't the first to record *Hey Joe*, but he made an indelible impression with it. It's a great and ominous song for when you're rearing your boy (or girl—*Hey Jo* will do just fine): "Hey, Joe, where you going with that (fill in the blank) in your hand?"

This way you teach him or her what ain't *cool*.

The Songs

Angel	*Angel*
Izabella	*Izabella*
Joe	*Hey Joe*
Mary	*Wind Cries Mary*

The Group

Jimi	Jimi Hendrix
Mitch	Mitch Mitchell
Noel	Noel Redding

Buddy Holly (and the Crickets)

If you're in love with Buddy Holly, the short-lived influential rocker, there are plenty of songs, even famous ones, for naming your baby.

If it's a girl, it's hard to imagine not naming her Peggy Sue. That's for a little girl who's *pretty pretty pretty pretty*.

The Songs

Bo	*Bo Diddley*
Don	*Modern Don Juan*
Holly	*Holly Hop*
Joe	*Smokey Joe's Café*
Ollie	*Rock Around with Ollie Vee*
Peggy Sue	*Peggy Sue*
	Peggy Sue Got Married
Teddy	*Ready Teddy*

The Group

Buddy	Buddy Holly
Jerry	Jerry Allison
Joe	Joe Maudlin
Niki	Niki Sullivan

John Lee Hooker

The Songs

Alberta	*Alberta*
Annie	*Annie Mae*
Dazie	*Dazie Mae*
Eloise	*Miss Eloise, Miss Eloise*
Henry	*Henry's Swing Club*
James	*I'm Bad Like Jesse James*
	Jesse James
John	*John L's House Rent Boogie*
	Johnny Lee's Mood
	Johnny Lee's Original Boogie
	Johnny Lee and the Thing
	Johnny Says Come Back
Lee	*Baby Lee*
Louise	*Louise*
Mae	*Annie Mae*
	Miss Sadie Mae
	Sally Mae
	Stella Mae
Maudie	*Maudie*
Sadie	*Miss Sadie Mae*
Sally	*Sally Mae*
	Mustang Sally and GTO
Stella	*Stella Mae*

Billy Idol

For all you Idol-worshippers, there aren't too many baby names in his songs.

Those available, though are fittingly dramatic. Once your boy is up and about, and destroying your sound system, you may well want to contain him, making *Adam in Chains* appropriate. For your girl, there's *Venus*. Phew.

The Songs

Adam	*Adam in Chains*
Venus	*Venus*

The Group

Billy	Billy Idol
Judi	Judi Dozier
Steve	Steve Stevens
	Steve Webster
Thommy	Thommy Price

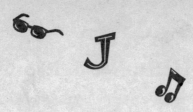

Jackson Five

The Motown group that made Michael Jackson a star produced a baby name classic: *Mama's Pearl*. Not only is Pearl a pretty name for your girl, but don't you think your daughter is precious, like a pearl?

The Songs

Jamie	*Jamie*
Pearl	*Mama's Pearl*

The Group

Jackie	Jackie Jackson
Jermaine	Jermaine Jackson
Marlon	Marlon Jackson
Michael	Michael Jackson
Tito	Tito Jackson

Michael Jackson

Some of these names are best ruled out—for instance, *Billie Jean* is probably not a good one, unless you're looking for a rockin' that's-*not*-my-baby name.

For big hit numbers, *Ben* works for a boy. For girls' names, *Dirty Diana* isn't such a bad idea—ever known a child who was perfectly clean on her own?

The Songs

Ben	*Ben*
Billie	*Billie Jean*
Diana	*Dirty Diana*
Jean	*Billie Jean*
Maria	*Maria (You Were the Only One)*
Robin	*Rockin' Robin*

Jefferson Airplane/ Starship

Well, *Jefferson*, or *Jeff*, aren't bad names right off the bat, if you want to name your baby for the band that first put acid rock on the charts way back when.

Martha is probably the most famous of the baby name candidates, and it's appropriate as well: by the time your child is two she'll be, as the song suggests, doing as she pleases, and this is a phase that commonly lasts about, oh, thirty years.

For a boy consider Fastbuck Freddie, from the Starship in-

Jefferson Airplane/ Starship (cont'd)

carnation of the group. Why not? Your boy could be quite the entrepreneur.

Trivia: On the subject of baby names, this group has already been in the news. In 1970, when Grace Slick was expecting Paul Kantner's child, they announced they were going to name the child *god* after everyone's favorite deity, only with a small *g*. Before little *god Slick* was born, however, the parents had a change of heart and settled on the name China.

The Airplane Songs

Alexander	*Alexander the Medium*
Alice	*White Rabbit*
Fredrick	*Hey Fredrick*
Martha	*Martha*
Miranda	*Crazy Miranda*

The Starship Songs

Caroline	*Caroline*
Charles	*St. Charles*
Freddie	*Fastbuck Freddie*

The Groups (selective)

Craig	Craig Chaquito
David	David Freiberg
Grace	Grace Slick
Jack	Jack Cassidy
John	Papa John Creech
	John Barbata
Jorma	Jorma Kakounen
Marty	Marty Balin
Paul	Paul Kantner
Pete	Pete Sears
Spencer	Spencer Dryden

Billy Joel

Piano Man fans will rejoice in the number of songs available. Tender songs, upbeat songs, angry songs, sardonic songs— you name it.

If you have a girl, probably the most distinctive name from his catalog is Rosalinda, as *Rosalinda's Eyes* may well perfectly express your sentiment for your girl.

The Songs

Angel	*Lullaby (Goodnight My Angel)*
Alexa	*The Downeaster "Alexa"*
Billy	*Ballad of Billy the Kid*
Christie	*Christie Lee*
Grace	*State of Grace*
Jack	*Captain Jack*
James	*James*
Judy	*Why Judy Why*
Laura	*Laura*
Leyna	*All for Leyna*
Roberta	*Roberta*
Rosalinda	*Rosalinda's Eyes*

Elton John

Fun names, goofy names, cute names—Elton John has them all in one of the best name catalogs in all of rock.

You don't even have to stick to easy ones like Jeannie or Bennie. Why not name your son Hercules? Or, to celebrate the end of the cold war . . . Nikita!

The Songs

Amy	*Amy*
Angeline	*Angeline*
Bennie	*Bennie and the Jets*
Billy	*Billy Bones and the White Bird*
Chloe	*Chloe*
Daniel	*The Ballad of Danny Bailey (1909-34)*
	Dan Dare (Pilot of the Future)
	Daniel
Dixie	*Dixie Lily*
Elton	*Elton's Song*
Emily	*Emily*
Georgie	*Georgie*
	Slow Down Georgie (She's Poison)
Greg	*Song for Greg*
Hercules	*Hercules*
Jean/Jeannie	*Little Jeannie*
John	*Johnny B. Goode*
	Dear John
	Empty Garden (Hey Hey Johnny)
Lisa	*Mona Lisas and Mad Hatters—Part Two*
Lucy	*Lucy in the Sky With diamonds*
Marlon	*Goodbye Marlon Brando*
Mona	*Mona Lisas and Mad Hatters—Part Two*
Norma Jean	*Candle in the Wind*
Nikita	*Nikita*
Pinky	*Pinky*
Roy	*Roy Rogers*
Suzie	*Suzie (Dramas)*

Rickie Lee Jones

The Songs

Chuck	*Chuck E's in Love*
Danny	*Danny's All-Star Joint*
Renee	*Walk Away Renee*
Stuart	*Stuart's Goat*
Woody	*Woody and Dutch on the Slow Train*

Tom Jones

The lounge-singin' blues man—Wayne Newton meets James Brown—managed more than a few hits in the rock era.

Delilah will work for naming a daughter. Just don't try belting it the way Tom Jones did—you may break something.

The Songs

Delilah	*Delilah*
Lucille	*Letter to Lucille*

Janis Joplin

(includes Big Brother and the Holding Company)

If your baby is like most, it was born with a set of lungs that may remind you of the late great Janis Joplin.

If so, why not name her Janis? If it's a boy, Bobby's a good choice, after the Pearl's only hit single, *Me and Bobby McGee*.

The Songs

Arthur	*Port Arthur High School*
Bobby	*Me and Bobby McGee*
Harry	*Harry*
Jane	*Mary Jane*
Jordon	*River Jordon*
Mary	*Mary Jane*
	O' Sweet Mary

The Group

Dave	Dave Getz
James	James Gurley
Janis	Janis Joplin
Pearl	Janis Joplin
Peter	Peter S. Albin
Sam	Sam Houston Andrew, III

Journey

The Songs

Angel   *City of Angels*
Suzanne   *Suzanne*

The Group

Aynsley   Aynsley Dunbar
Gregg   Gregg Rolie
Jonathan   Jonathan Cain
Larrie   Larrie Londin
Neal   Neal Schon
Randy   Randy Jackson
Ross   Ross Valory
Steve   Steve Perry
                 Steve Smith

Carole King

If you idolize songwriters, you can immortalize them in your little girl by naming her Carole, after Carole King, the hit songwriter who also has had a notable solo career.

The Songs

Ambrosia	*Ambrosia*
Jack	*Smackwater Jack*
Johnny	*One Was Johnny*
Joy	*Wrap Around Joy*
Rosie	*Really Rosie*

Kinks

The enduring and witty British group left its permanent mark on girl names with its smash hit *Lola* (pronounced Lo-lo-lo-lo-Lola).

There are candidates in their opus for boy names too, but the best ones might be from the group itself.

The Songs

Annabella	*Annabella*
Arthur	*Arthur*
David	*David Watts*
Harry	*Harry Rag*
Johnny	*Johnny Thunder*
Lola	*Lola*
Monica	*Monica*
Polly	*Polly*
Susannah	*Susannah's Still Alive*
Victoria	*Victoria*

The Group

Dave	Dave Davies
John	John Dalton
	John Gosling
Mick	Mick Avory
Peter	Peter Quaife
Ray	Ray Davies

Kiss

You may be secretly wishing your baby would come out of the womb wearing glittery (and scary) makeup. If so, you have a Kiss baby. For girls, there are several songs to choose from, especially the group's rare tender moment *Beth*. For boys, there's the group.

The Songs

Beth	*Beth*
Caesar	*Little Caesar*
Christine	*Christine Sixteen*
Domino	*Domino*
Shandi	*Shandi*

Kiss (cont'd)

The Group

Ace	Ace Frehley
Gene	Gene Simmons
Paul	Paul Stanley
Pete	Pete Criss

Kool and the Gang

The Songs

Joanna	*Joanna*

The Group

Claydes	Claydes Smith
D.T.	Dennis (D. T.) Thomas
Dennis	Dennis (D. T.) Thomas
George	George Brown
Khalis	Khalis Bayyan
Kool	Robert (Kool) Bell
Rick	Rick West
Robert	Robert (Kool) Bell
	Robert (Spike) Mickens

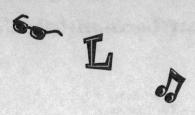

Labelle

The Songs

Danny   *Danny Boy*
Johnny   *When Johnny Comes Marching Home*
Joy   *Joy to Have Your Love*

The Group

Nona   Nona Hendryx
Patti   Patti LaBelle
Sarah   Sarah Dash

John Lennon

First, if it's Lennon you want to honor, don't forget the Lennon-penned Beatles songs, such as *Lucy in the Sky with Diamonds*, *Julia*, and *Sexy Sadie*.

But if it's solo Lennon you want, use the list below. (If you choose Yoko, you are one true fan.)

John Lennon (cont'd)

The Songs

Angel	*Angel Baby*
	I'm Your Angel
Angela	*Angela*
John	*John Sinclair*
Lucie	*Bring on the Lucie (Freeda People)*
Peggy	*Peggy Sue*
Sue	*Peggy Sue*
Teddy	*Ready Teddy*
Yoko	*Dear Yoko*
	Oh Yoko!

Led Zeppelin

If you have a peripatetic little guy, you may consider *Walter's Walk* or even, if he's inclined to dance, *Boogie with Stu*.
  For girls, it has to be *Darlene*.

The Songs

Bonzo	*Bonzo's Montreux*
Darlene	*Darlene*
Dick	*Moby Dick*
Kashmir	*Kashmir*
Roy	*Hats Off to Roy Harper*
Stu	*Boogie with Stu*
Tom	*Pool Tom*
Walter	*Walter's Walk*

The Group

Jimmy	Jimmy Page
John	John Bonham
	John Paul Jones
Paul	John Paul Jones
Robert	Robert Plant

Annie Lennox

(*see* Eurythmics)

Huey Lewis and the News

The Songs

Lee	*Stagger Lee*

The Group

Bill	Bill Gibson
Chris	Chris Hayes
Huey	Huey Lewis
Johnny	Johnny Colla
Mario	Mario Cipollina
Sean	Sean Hopper

Little Feat

The band with the little name and the big guitarist (the late Lowell George) produced one great tune for naming a boy: *Crazy Captain Gunboat Willie*. Why not name him the entire title? By the time he can say his own name, he'll be ready to recite the Preamble of the Constitution.

The Songs

Juliette	*Juliette*
Willie	*Crazy Captain Gunboat Willie*

The Group

Bill	Bill Payne
Kenny	Kenny Gradney
Lowell	Lowell George
Paul	Paul Barrere
Richard	Richard Hayward
Roy	Roy Estrada
Sam	Sam Clayton

Little Richard

Oh, *baby!* If you think the antics of this part-time singer, part-time evangelist are extreme, wait until you see the histrionics your child is capable of! Which, of course, makes Little Richard a fine inspiration for naming your baby—not to mention the galaxy of great, great songs, like *Lucille*, *Good Golly Miss Molly*, and *Long Tall Sally*.

The Songs

Ann	*Miss Ann*
Annie	*Annie is Back*
Irene	*Goodnight Irene*
Jenny	*Jenny, Jenny*
Lucille	*Lucille*
Molly	*Good Golly Miss Molly*
Sally	*Long Tall Sally*
Suzy	*Groovy Little Suzy*
Teddy	*Ready Teddy*

Kenny Loggins

(*see also* Loggins and Messina)

The footloose singer has many great female name songs. If you have a boy, it's going to have to be Kenny.

The Songs

Angelique	*Angelique*
Cody	*Cody's Song*
Faith	*Leap of Faith*
Isabella	*Isabella's Eyes*
Judy	*St. Judy's Comet*
Lorraine	*Lorraine*

Loggins and Messina

(*see also* Kenny Loggins)

The Songs

Christopher	*House at Pooh Corner*
Danny	*Danny's Song*
Georgia	*Back to Georgia*
Lahaina	*Lahaina*
Marie	*Sweet Marie*
Robin	*House at Pooh Corner*

The Group

Jim	Jim Messina
Kenny	Kenny Loggins

Los Lobos

This crossover band brought rock with a Spanish bent to the mainstream airwaves. Plus—lucky for you—no shortage of songs for naming your child, whether you want a Spanish bent or not.

The Songs

Angel	*Angel Dance*
	Angels with Dirty Faces
Bertha	*Bertha*
Emily	*Emily*
Evangelini	*Evangelini*
Georgia	*Georgia Slop*
Jane	*Two Janes*
Jenny	*Jenny's Got a Pony*
John	*Little John of God*
Kiko	*Kiko and the Lavender Moon*
Maria	*Bella Maria de Mi Alma*
Reva	*Reva's House*

The Group

Cesar	Cesar Rosas
Conrad	Conrad Lozano
David	David Hidalgo
Louie	Louie Perez
Steve	Steve Berlin
Victor	Victor Bisetti

Lynyrd Skynyrd

The great southern band with only Welsh vowels offers a few songs for naming your baby.

To take this all the way—that is, to fully honor the group—you may want to alter the spellings slightly, say, to Cyrtys, Gyrgyy, and Myssy.

Then again, maybe not.

The Songs

Curtis	*Ballad of Curtis Love*
Georgia	*Georgia Peaches*
Missy	*Sweet Little Missy*

The Group

Allen	Allen Collins
Artimus	Artimus Pyle
Billy	Billy Powell
Ed	Ed King
Gary	Gary Rossington
Leon	Leon Wilkeson
Ronnie	Ronnie Van Zant

Madonna

Well, if Madonna can have a baby, you can certainly name a baby after Madonna. (Airtight logic, right?) And Madonna itself is a perfectly fine name for a girl—why not?

If it's a material *boy* you've brought into this material world, consider Jessie and Jimmy.

The Songs

Angel	*Angel*
Jessie	*Dear Jessie*
Jimmy	*Jimmy Jimmy*

Paul McCartney (and Wings)

Remember that there are many Paul songs (credited to Lennon and McCartney) in the Beatles catalog, great baby-name songs like *Michelle* and *Martha My Dear*.

Paul McCartney
(and Wings) (cont'd)

But if you're insistent on the solo McCartney there are several songs to choose from, including those from big hits like Helen (*Wheels*) and (*Uncle*) Albert.

The Songs

Albert	*Uncle Albert/Admiral Halsey*
Clawdy	*Lawdy Miss Clawdy*
Helen	*Helen Wheels*
Junior	*Junior's Farm*
Linda	*Lovely Linda*
Lucille	*Lucille*
Sally	*Sally*
Teddy	*Teddy Boy*

The Group

Denny	Denny Laine
Jimmy	Jimmy McCulloch
Joe	Joe English
Linda	Linda McCartney
Paul	Paul McCartney

Metallica

It's shocking, but this group—which produces nothing but the tenderest of music, tunes that often flirt with being overly slushy and sentimental—has produced *no obvious baby name songs!* Yes, it's a shock.

So, if you want to name your child after this group, you'll have to go to the group names themselves. If you have a girl, it's going to have to be Metallica. (Good luck explaining to your parents.)

The Songs

None!

The Group

James	James Hetfield
Jason	Jason Newsted
Kirk	Kirk Hammett
Lars	Lars Ulrich

George Michael

(includes Wham!)

Where there's life, there's hope. Where there's hope, there's faith. And where there's *Faith*, there's George Michael (shaking his butt like there's no tomorrow).

If your daughter is this kind of faith, then name her Faith. If it's a boy, then maybe he's a boy George.

The Songs

Angel	*Cowboys and Angels*
Faith	*Faith*
Ray	*Ray of Sunshine*

The Group (Wham!)

Andrew	Andrew Ridgely
George	George Michael
Georgios	Georgios Panayiotou

Steve Miller

The Songs

Fanny	*Fanny Mae*
Grace	*Your Saving Grace*
Jackson	*Jackson Kent Blues*
Kent	*Jackson Kent Blues*
Mary	*Dear Mary*
Steve	*Steve Miller's Midnight Tango*

Joni Mitchell

A generation ago, Bill and Hillary Clinton didn't need this book, because they knew all along how to name a baby, which, of course, is after a song. Hence, Chelsea Clinton, named after Joni's *Chelsea Morning*.

Joni provides a great variety of songs, whether your daughter is the only Joy in town, or is a Michael from the mountains.

The Songs

Amelia	*Amelia*
Angel	*Tin Angel*
Carey	*Carey*
Chelsea	*Chelsea Morning*
Don	*Don Juan's Reckless Daughter*
Edith	*Edith and the Kingpin*
Harry	*Harry's House*
Joy	*Only Joy in Town*
Louise	*Cherokee Louise*

Magdalene	*Magdalene Laundries*
Marcie	*Marcie*
Michael	*Michael From Mountains*
Nathan	*Nathan La Franeer*
Rose	*Roses Blue*
	For the Roses
Willy	*Willy*
Yvette	*Yvette in English*

Moody Blues

Once your child is a teenager, you may wish you'd named him or her Moody. Don't do it! Give the child time . . . most grow out of it (eventually).

Your child is more effectively named if you choose Emily, for a girl, or one of the group names if it's a boy.

The Songs

Emily	*Emily's Song*

The Group

Graeme	Graeme Edge
John	John Lodge
Justin	Justin Hayward
Mike	Mike Pinder
Ray	Ray Thomas

Van Morrison

For girls, it's hard to argue with the classic *Gloria*, in which you not only get to sing the praises of your girl, but you can teach her how to spell her name.

For boys, there are many less known choices. *Rave On, John Donne* has its appeal—your baby/child/teenager will be raving here and there, and you may just want to fight fire with fire.

The Songs

Alan	*Alan Watts Blues*
Angel	*Contacting My Angel*
	Across the Bridge Where the Angels Dwell
Angeliou	*Angeliou (Into the Music)*
George	*Madame George*
Gloria	*Gloria*
Jackie	*Jackie Wilson Said*
Jannie	*Sweet Jannie*
Joe	*Joe Harper Saturday Morning*
Joey	*I'm Tired Joey Boy*
John	*Rave On, John Donne*
Ray	*Celtic Ray*
Rose	*Spanish Rose*
	Ro Ro Rosey

Mötley Crüe

The Songs

Angela	*Angela*
Jack	*Uncle Jack*
Nona	*Nona*

The Group

Mick	Mick Mars
Nikki	Nikki Sixx
Tommy	Tommy Lee
Vince	Vince Neil

Willie Nelson

Of course your child is always going to be on your mind . . .
Country Willie has thankfully provided many names to have
on your mind, too.

The Songs

Angel	*Angel Flying Too Close to the Ground*
Buddy	*Buddy*
Charlie	*Goodtime Charlie's Got the Blues*
Georgia	*Georgia on My Mind*
Grace	*Amazing Grace*
Jimmy	*Jimmy's Road*
Mona	*Mona Lisa*
Pancho	*Pancho and Lefty*
Paul	*Me and Paul*
Rose	*Summer Roses*
Rosetta	*Rosetta*
Willie	*Country Willie*

Randy Newman

As much as you may love this great songwriter and singer, you may agree that a lot of his songs are, well, not exactly appropriate for naming a baby. For instance, no matter how cute and pudgy your son is, *Davy the Fat Boy* is probably a bad idea.

Mr. Newman, though, has his tender and fun side. *Linda* is a lovely love song, and *Simon Smith and the Amazing Dancing Bear* is awfully fun, too.

The Songs

Annabelle	*Annabelle/Annabelle Toodleoo*
Bob	*Uncle Bob's Midnight Blues*
Bret	*Oh Bret*
	Bret Escapes
	Bret's Card/Sore Loser
Davy	*Davy the Fat Boy*
Kathleen	*Kathleen (Catholicism Made Easier)*
Joseph	*Joseph and the Russian*
Linda	*Linda*
Lucinda	*Lucinda*
Marie	*Marie*
Mikey	*Mikey's*
Rosemary	*Rosemary*
Simon	*Simon Smith and the Amazing Dancing Bear*
Suzanne	*Suzanne*

Nirvana

In the broad category of "Groups your mother wouldn't want
you to name your child after," Nirvana is high on the list. No
matter—this is *your* baby.

Who knows—you may come from a long line of fine hair-
cutters, so Floyd is a perfectly fitting name. Just don't tell
mom.

The Songs

Floyd	*Floyd the Barber*
Penny	*Penny Royal Tea*
Polly	*Polly*

The Group

Chad	Chad Channing
Chris	Chris Novoselic
David	David Grohl
Jason	Jason Everman
Kurt	Kurt Cobain
Pat	Pat Smear

Roy Orbison

The mild-mannered Roy Orbison didn't supply many boy names, so for a son, it's Roy or nothing.

For a girl, there's a slew of fine songs. The famous *Leah* offers a sweet tale of a love for a Leah so strong that she's worth diving deep in search of pearls. And *Claudette* is perfect for any pretty little girl—especially yours.

The Songs

Angel	*Blue Angel*
Belinda	*Belinda*
Candy	*Candy Man*
Claudette	*Claudette*
Gloria	*Going Back to Gloria*
Jolie	*Jolie*
Lana	*Lana*
Leah	*Leah*

Pearl Jam

Up there with Nirvana in the groups-your-mother-wouldn't-want-you-to-name-your-child-after category. And it's hard to imagine anyone, even the direst of Pearl Jam fans, naming a son after the song *Jeremy*, but hey, this book offers only choices and does not pass judgment!

For girls, there's only one obvious choice . . . Pearl.

The Songs

| Davanita | *Aye, Davanita* |
| Jeremy | *Jeremy* |

The Group

Dave	Dave Abbruzzese
	Dave Krusen
Eddie	Eddie Vedder
Jack	Jack Irons
Jeff	Jeff Ament
Mike	Mike McCready
Pearl	Pearl Jam
Stone	Stone Gossard

Pet Shop Boys

The Songs

| Don | *Don Juan* |
| Jack | *Jack the Lad* |

The Group

| Chris | *Chris Lowe* |
| Neil | *Neil Tennant* |

Tom Petty and the Heartbreakers

One look in your little girl's eyes, and you may be tempted to name her Heartbreaker. And during their snitty phases when they're older, you may wish for a moment you'd named him or her Petty.

Restraint is advised! You'll never regret it if you opt for names like Tom and Mary Jane.

The Songs

Jane	*Mary Jane's Last Dance*
Magnolia	*Magnolia*
Mary	*Mary Jane's Last Dance*
	Mary's New Car

Tom Petty and the Heartbreakers (cont'd)

The Group

Benmont	Benmont Tench
Howie	Howie Epstein
Mike	Mike Campbell
Stan	Stan Lynch
Tom	Tom Petty

Pink Floyd

Lots o' great candidates here.

Pink Floyd fans of Irish heritage may love the option of Seamus. If you have a playful little girl, there's *See Emily Play*. If you have a son who's considerably less playful, consider *Careful with that Axe, Eugene*.

The Songs

Alan	*Alan's Psychedelic Breakfast*
Arnold	*Arnold Layne*
Emily	*See Emily Play*
Eugene	*Careful with that Axe, Eugene*
Fletcher	*The Fletcher Memorial Home*
Julia	*Julia Dream*
Sam	*Lucifer Sam*
Seamus	*Seamus*
Vera	*Vera*

The Group

David	David Gilmour
Floyd	Pink Floyd

Nick	Nick Mason
Rick	Rick Wright
Roger	Roger Waters
Syd	Syd Barrett

Poco

The Songs

Angel	*Angel*
Brenda	*Brenda X*
Faith	*Faith in the Families*
Magnolia	*Magnolia*
Rocky	*Rocky Mountain Breakdown*

The Group

Charlie	Charlie Harrison
Kim	Kim Bullard
Paul	Paul Cotton
Rusty	Rusty Young
Steve	Steve Chapman

Police

(includes Sting)

Be warned: if you name your daughter Roxanne, people will be singing "ROX-anne!" in her general direction for the rest of her life.

Lolita is a subtle choice if you think you're having a girl who'll entice inappropriately old men—you know, men just like "that old man in that book by Nabokov," as the song goes.

The Songs

Agnes	*Saint Agnes and the Burning Train*
Angel	*When the Angels Fall*
Jeremiah	*The Jeremiah Blues Part I*
Lolita	*Don't Stand So Close to Me*
Roxanne	*Roxanne*
Sally	*Be My Girl—Sally*

The Group

Andy	Andy Summers
Stewart	Stewart Copeland
Sting	Sting

Iggy Pop

Well, why not Iggy??

It's a perfect name, and your grandmother will *love* it (cough).

The Songs

Caesar	*Caesar*
Louie	*Louie Louie*

The Group

Hunt	Hunt Sales
Iggy	Iggy Pop
Ricky	Ricky Gardiner
Scott	Scott Thurston
Stacey	Stacey Heydon
Tony	Tony Sales

Elvis Presley

If you've ruled out, for boys, Elvis, Aron, and Colonel Tom, and for girls, Priscilla, Kathy Lee, Dru, and Elvis, then you still have a heap of baby name songs to choose from for your little King.

Of the songs associated with Elvis exclusively, probably the most famous baby name song is *Teddy Bear (Let Me Be Your)*. And what better song? Appropriate for the baby, for the bear you get, for the parents themselves. One big cuddly family.

The Songs

Abraham	*Bosom of Abraham*
Adam	*Adam and Evil*
Angel	*Angel*
Annie	*Polk Salad Annie*
Carnie	*Carny Town*
Caroline	*Sweet Caroline*
Charro	*Charro!*
Clawdy	*Lawdy Miss Clawdy*
Danny	*Danny*
Grace	*Amazing Grace*
Jack	*From a Jack to a King*

Elvis Presley (cont'd)

The Songs

Jim	*Just Tell Her Jim Said Hello*
Joe	*Stay Away, Joe*
John	*Johnny B. Goode*
	I, John
	Frankie/Johnny
Joshua	*Joshua Fit/Fought the Battle of Jericho*
Jude	*Hey Jude*
Judy	*Judy*
Marguerita	*Marguerita*
Marie	*His Latest Flame*
Mary	*Proud Mary*
	Mary in the Morning
Maybelline	*Maybelline*
Petunia	*Petunia, the Gardener's Daughter*
Sally	*Long Tall Sally*
Susan	*Susan When She Tried*
Sylvia	*Sylvia*
Teddy	*Teddy Bear (Let Me Be Your)*
	Ready Teddy Violet
Violet	*Violet (Live a Little Love a Little)*

Pretenders

No name songs here. But if you want to honor the group's admirable leader, name your girl Chrissie.

The Songs

None!

The Group

Chrissie	Chrissie Hynde

Prince

If you want to pay homage to this rock icon, you could name your baby "The Child Formerly Known as Prince." (It's not recommended, but you could.)

Be careful with some of these names—they're included for the sake of completeness, but some are about as appropriate for naming your child as taking him or her to an X-rated movie.

The Songs

Anna	*Anna Stasia*
Annie	*Annie Christian*
Billy	*Billy Jack Bitch*
Bob	*Bob George*
Christian	*Annie Christian*
Christopher	*Christopher Tracy's Song*
Cindy	*Cindy C.*
George	*Bob George*
Jack	*Jack U Off*
	Billy Jack Bitch
Joy	*Joy in Repetition*
Nikki	*Darling Nikki*
Pearl	*Diamonds and Pearls*
Ronnie	*Ronnie, Talk to Russia*
Tracy	*Christopher Tracy's Song*
Venus	*Venus de Milo*

Queen

If you're a *Wayne's World* fan *and* a Queen fan, you can honor both in one fell swoop with the name Galileo, from the group's very subtle (*not*) hit *Bohemian Rhapsody,* featured memorably in *Wayne's World*. Mama mia!

The Songs

Delilah	*Delilah*
Galileo	*Bohemian Rhapsody*
Lilly	*Lilly of the Valley*
Mary Lou	*Hello Mary Lou (Goodbye Heart)*
Mia	*Bohemian Rhapsody*

The Group

Brian	Brian May
Freddie	Freddie Mercury
John	John Deacon
Roger	Roger Taylor

Bonnie Raitt

The Songs

Angel	*Angel*
	Angel From Montgomery
Chico	*Papa Come Quick (Jody and Chico)*
Jody	*Papa Come Quick (Jody and Chico)*
Louise	*Louise*

Ramones

If it's a girl, it's got to be Ramona—why, the name practically *sounds* like the group.

For a boy, the first name doesn't really matter. With this group, it's the *last* name that counts, and it has to be Ramone.

The Songs

Danny	*Danny Says*
Heidi	*Heidi Is a Headache*
Jackie	*The Return of Jackie and Judy*

Ramones (cont'd)

The Songs

Judy	*Judy is a Punk*
	The Return of Jackie and Judy
Ramona	*Ramona*
Sheena	*Sheena is a Punk Rocker*
Suzy	*Suzy is a Headbanger*

The Group

C.J.	C.J. Ramone
Dee Dee	Dee Dee Ramone
Joey	Joey Ramone
Johnny	Johnny Ramone
Marky	Marky Ramone
Ritchie	Ritchie Ramone
Tommy	Tommy Ramone

Red Hot Chili Peppers

The Songs

Johnny	*Johnny, Kick a Hole in the Sky*
Venus	*Subway to Venus*

The Group

Anthony	Anthony Keidis
Chad	Chad Smith
Dave	Dave Navarro
Flea	Michael Peter ''Flea'' Balzary
Hillel	Hillel Slovak
Jack	Jack Irons
Michael	Michael Peter ''Flea'' Balzary
Peter	Michael Peter ''Flea'' Balzary

Lou Reed

(see also Velvet Underground)

The monotone vocal singer and writer's best name song may
be the famous *Sweet Jane*.

Your child is sweet, right?

The Songs

Andy	*Andy's Chest*
Caroline	*Caroline Says (I and II)*
Dorita	*Dorita—the Spirit*
Harry	*Harry's Circumcision—Reverie Gone Astray*
Jane	*Sweet Jane*
Jim	*Oh Jim*
Juliet	*Romeo and Juliet*
Romeo	*Romeo and Juliet*
Sally	*Sally Can't Dance*

R. E. M.

For boys, *Voice of Harold* at least has a good title. It's appropriate: you'll be hearing a *lot* of baby Harold's voice.

No songs for girls, unfortunately. You can always get creative with initials, though: name her something like Reba Emily Martha.

R. E. M. (cont'd)

The Songs

Harold	*Voice of Harold*
Wendell	*Wendell Gee*

The Group

Bill	Bill Berry
Mike/Michael	Michael Stipe
	Mike Mills
Peter	Peter Buck

REO Speedwagon

The Songs

None!

The Group

Alan	Alan Gratzer
Gary	Gary Richrath
Greg	Greg Philbin
Michael	Michael Murphy
Neal	Neal Doughty

Rolling Stones

There's no lack of songs for naming your baby from the most enduring rock group ever. There are even lots of hits (for boys *and* girls): *Angie, Jumpin' Jack Flash, Lady Jane, Ruby Tuesday*.

The Songs

Amanda	*Miss Amanda Jones*
Angel	*Sweet Black Angel*
Angie	*Angie*
Carol	*Carol*
Fanny	*Jiving Sister Fanny*
Jack	*Jumpin' Jack Flash*
Jane	*Lady Jane*
Johnny	*Bye Bye Johnny*
Mona	*Mona*
Negrita	*Hey Negrita*
Ruby	*Ruby Tuesday*
Susie	*Susie Q*
Virginia	*Sweet Virginia*

The Group

Bill	Bill Wyman
Brian	Brian Jones
Charlie	Charlie Watts
Keith	Keith Richards
Mick	Mick Jagger
Ron	Ron Wood

Linda Ronstadt

The pop-rock singer, who has segued into adult contemporary, offers a few songs for naming a little girl (who, of course, can always be named Linda).

For boys, go with Angel (baby).

The Songs

Angel	*Angel Baby*
Carmelita	*Carmelita*
Louise	*Louise*
Shelly	*Some of Shelly's Blues*

Roxy Music

The Songs

Angel	*Angel Eyes*
Bob	*The Bob (Medley)*
Tara	*Tara*

The Group

Andrew	Andrew Mackay
Brian	Brian Eno
Bryan	Bryan Ferry
Paul	Paul Thompson
Phil	Phil Manzanera

Todd Rundgren

Aaron is *not* recommended, unless you have a *very* harsh attitude about toilet training. Come on, there are better choices here!

The Songs

Aaron	*Piss Aaron*
Denny	*The Ballad of Denny and Jean*
Jack	*Wolfman Jack*
Jean	*The Ballad of Denny and Jean*
Johnee	*Johnee Jingo*
Lili	*Lili's Address*
Marlene	*Marlene*

Rush

The Songs

Jacob	*Jacob's Ladder*
Jim	*Kristen and Jim*
Kristen	*Kristen and Jim*
Tom	*Tom Sawyer*
Walter	*Walter's Blues*
Will	*Will Gaines*
	Free Will

Rush (cont'd)

The Group

Alex	Alex Lifeson
Geddy	Geddy Lee
Neil	Neil Peart

Leon Russell

The Songs

Dixie	*Dixie Lullaby*
Eric	*Jammin' With Eric*
Hollis	*The Ballad of Hollis Brown*
Jack	*Jumping Jack Flash*
Jane	*Me and Baby Jane*
Lisa	*Mona Lisa Please*
Mona	*Mona Lisa Please*

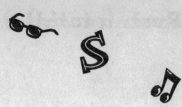

Sade

The smooth, smokey-voiced Sade featured female names in several melancholy tunes, like Jezebel and Maureen, which are suitable for a complex, *deep* little girl. For a boy, you may just want to name him Smooth Operator.

The Songs

Frankie	*Frankie's First Affair*
Jezebel	*Jezebel*
Maureen	*Maureen*
Sally	*Sally*

Santana

For a boy, it looks like it has to be Carlos (other group members are not noted; the personnel has changed frequently).

For girls, there are several songs, especially if you want to give your little *Chiquita* a name with some Spanish flavor.

Santana (cont'd)

The Songs

Angela	*Free Angela*
Faith	*Faith Interlude*
Hannibal	*Hannibal*
Maria	*Maria Caracoles*
Rose	*Spanish Rose*

Seal

Everyone's favorite singer named for an aquatic mammal. (The singers Whale and Walrus haven't gone *anywhere*.)

You will certainly like having a kiss from your little girl now and then . . . so name her Rose.

The Songs

Rose	*Kiss From a Rose*
Violet	*Violet*

Bob Seger

The Songs

Betty Lou	*Betty Lou's Gettin' Out Tonight*
Bo	*Bo Diddley*
Jody	*Jody Girl*
Mary Lou	*Mary Lou*

Carly Simon

If you think your child is going to have an ego problem, i.e., an overly enlarged one, *You're So Vain*, Carly's slap at Warren Beatty, could keep him in check.

The Songs

Angel	*Angel From Montgomery*
Dan	*Dan, My Fling*
Danny	*Danny Boy*
Davy	*Davy*
James	*James*
Jesse	*Jesse*
Julie	*Julie Through the Glass*
Libby	*Libby*
Orpheus	*Orpheus*
Warren	*You're So Vain*

Paul Simon

(*see also* Simon and Garfunkel)

There may be fifty ways to leave your lover, but there are only sixteen songs for naming your song after Paul Simon.

There are good ones, too, such as *You Can Call Me Al*, which your child can sing back to *you*.

The Songs

Al	*You Can Call Me Al*
Duncan	*Duncan*

Paul Simon (cont'd)

The Songs

Georgette	*Rene and Georgette Magritte with their Dog After the War*
Gus	*Fifty Ways to Leave Your Lover*
Jack	*Fifty Ways to Leave Your Lover*
Johnny	*The Late Great Johnny Ace*
Judy	*St. Judy's Comet*
Julio	*Me and Julio Down by the Schoolyard*
Lee	*Fifty Ways to Leave Your Lover*
Rene	*Rene and Georgette Magritte with their Dog After the War*
Roy	*Fifty Ways to Leave Your Lover*
Stan	*Fifty Ways to Leave Your Lover*

Simon and Garfunkel

(*see also* Paul Simon)

Lots of classic sixties songs here, especially for girls: *Cecilia; For Emily, Whenever I May Find Her; Kathy's Song.*
For boys, the best bets may be Paul and Artie.

The Songs

Anji	*Anji*
April	*April Come She Will*
Cecilia	*Cecilia*
Emily	*For Emily, Whenever I May Find Her*
Frank	*So Long, Frank Lloyd Wright*
Kathy	*Kathy's Song*

Lloyd	*So Long, Frank Lloyd Wright*
Peggy	*Peggy-O*
Richard	*Richard Cory*
Tom	*The Only Living Boy in New York*

The Group

| Art/Arthur | Art Garfunkel |
| Paul | Paul Simon |

Sly and the Family Stone

The Songs

| Jane | *Jane is a Groupie* |
| Jim | *Plastic Jim* |

The Group

Cynthia	Cynthia Robinson
Freddie	Freddie "Stone" Stewart
Greg	Greg Errico
Jerry	Jerry Martini
Larry	Larry Graham, Jr.
Rosie	Rosie "Stone" Stewart
Sylvester	Sylvester "Sly Stone" Stewart
Sly	Sylvester "Sly Stone" Stewart

Smiths

The Songs

Marie	*His Latest Flame*
Sheila	*Sheila Take a Bow*
William	*William, It was Really Nothing*

The Group

Andy	Andy Rourke
Johnny	Johnny Marr
Mike	Mike Joyce
Morrissey	Morrissey

Spencer Davis Group

(*see* Steve Winwood)

Spinners

If you think of the seventies as a fun era when everyone was having a good time dancing to good-time music, you probably fondly remember the Spinners, with their close harmonies and upbeat tunes.

For girl names, choose from their songs. For boys, use the members of the group.

The Songs

Allison	*Memories of Allison*
Sadie	*Sadie*
Susan	*Lazy Susan*
Susie	*Wake Up Susie*

The Group

Billy	Billy Henderson
Bobbie	Bobbie Smith
Henry	Henry Fambrough
Pervis	Pervis Jackson
Philippe	Philippe Soul Wynne

Bruce Springsteen

If you're a Springsteen fan, chances are you're going to have a baby who's *boss*, and needs to be named accordingly.

There's no shortage of good names. Maybe you have a little girl with dazzling peepers (*Gloria's Eyes*) or one who's particularly darling (*Sherry Darling*). Name your girl Rosalita and you've got a Bruce signature name as well as a perennial excuse to coax a shy one out of her shell.

For boys, there's Johnny, Billy, Adam, and even—if you insist—Cain.

The Songs

Adam	*Adam Raised a Cain*
Angel	*Angel*
Billy	*Wild Billy's Curious Story*

Bruce Springsteen (cont'd)

The Songs

Bobby Jean	*Bobby Jean*
Cain	*Adam Raised a Cain*
Candy	*Candy's Room*
Gloria	*Gloria's Eyes*
Jackson	*Jackson Cage*
Johnny	*Johnny 99*
Kitty	*Kitty's Back*
Mary	*Mary Queen of Arkansas*
Rosalita	*Rosalita (Come Out Tonight)*
Sandy	*4th of July, Asbury Park (Sandy)*
Sherry	*Sherry Darling*
Tom	*Ghost of Tom Joad*
Wendy	*Born to Run*

Squeeze

The Songs

Annie	*Annie Get Your Gun*
Daphne	*Daphne*
George	*King George Street*

The Group

Chris	Chris Difford
Gilson	Gilson Lavis
Glenn	Glenn Tilbrook
John	John Bentley
Keith	Keith Wilkinson
Kevin	Kevin Wilkinson
Paul	Paul Carrack

Steely Dan

Given that reading Steely Dan lyrics is like being handed a few random pages from *Finnegan's Wake*, it may seem hard to find Steely baby names that make any sense.

Still, there's always the more-accessible-than-average *Josie*, for the so-good baby who's the pride of your neighborhood. And *Rose Darling*, a non-hit from *Katy Lied*, is as sweet and uncomplicated as anything they've done.

As for the others—does anyone alive have a clue what *Aja* is about? Or *Peg*? If parenthood is *confusing* to you, these could be good names.

Trivia: Yes, you could always name a child Dan. You should know, though, that the group name Steely Dan was inspired by a *metallic dildo*. (Still like Dan?)

The Songs

Aja	*Aja*
Barry	*Barrytown*
Charlie	*Charlie Freak*
Jack	*Do it Again*
Josie	*Josie*
Pearl	*Pearl of the Quarter*
Parker	*Parker's Band*
Peg	*Peg*
Rikki	*Rikki Don't Lose that Number*
Rose	*Rose Darling*

The Group

Dan	Steely Dan
David	David Palmer
Denny	Denny Dias
Donald	Donald Fagan
Jeff	Jeff "Skunk" Baxter
Jim	Jim Hodder
Skunk	Jeff "Skunk" Baxter
Walter	Walter Becker

Steppenwolf

It's bound to feel at times that *any* baby you might have, be it boy or girl, is basically *born to be wild*. You may already be worrying about what's going to happen when your kid is a teenager.

If so, name the tyke after the sixties band with the literary name that sounded like an *Easy Rider* soundtrack. There are oodles of songs for boys and girls alike.

The Songs

Berry	*Berry Rides Again*
Caroline	*Caroline (Are You Ready for the Outside World)*
Corina	*Corina, Corina*
Jack	*Fat Jack*
Penny	*Mr. Penny Pincher*
Sam	*Don't Step on the Grass, Sam*

The Group

George	George Biando
Goldie	Goldie McJohn
Jerry	Jerry Edmonton
John	John Kay
Kent	Kent Henry
Mars	Mars Bonfire
Nick	Nick St. Nicholas

Rod Stewart

(includes Faces, Small Faces)

If you've got a brand new boy who's bound to make ya think he's sexy, you may want to name him after the veteran rocker who first popularized the just-got-shocked hairdo. You could name the baby Rod or after any number of songs from Mr. Stewart's catalog.

If you have a girl, the most obvious choice is Maggie, after the megahit *Maggie May*.

The Songs

Angel	*Angel*
Christopher	*Hang on St. Christopher*
Cindy	*Cindy's Lament*
Dixie	*Dixie Toot*
Georgie	*Killing of Georgie (Part I and II)*
Grace	*Amazing Grace*
Jane	*Baby Jane*
Jo	*Jo's Lament*
Jodie	*Jodie*
Judy	*Miss Judy's Farm*
Maggie	*Maggie May*
Mary	*Sweet Lady Mary*
Matilda	*Tom Traubert's Blues (Waltzing Matilda)*
Muddy	*Muddy, Sam, and Otis*
Otis	*Muddy, Sam, and Otis*
Sam	*Muddy, Sam, and Otis*
Sonny	*Sonny*
Tom	*Tom Traubert's Blues (Waltzing Matilda)*
Virginia	*Leave Virginia Alone*

Rod Stewart (cont'd)

The Group

Ian	Ian McLagan
Kenney	Kenney Jones
Rod	Rod Stewart
Ron	Ron Wood
Ronnie	Ronnie Lane

Sting

(*see* Police)

Supertramp

Best avoid Mary and Jane if you're naming your girl after this group—those names were used none too flatteringly in the song *Goodbye Stranger*.

The songs below offer a few names for girls; for boys, there's Rudy or the members of the group.

The Songs

Bonnie	*Bonnie*
Rosie	*Rosie Had Everything Planned*
Rudy	*Rudy*

The Group

Anthony	John Anthony Helliwell
Bob	Bob C. Benberg
Dougie	Dougie Thomson
John	John Anthony Helliwell
Richard	Richard Davies
Roger	Roger Hodgson

Talking Heads

Let's hope for your sake that your baby will never be burning down your house. In addition, you'll probably want him or her to always be lucid and rational—that is, to never stop making sense.

Still, you may want to immortalize this group anyway. Band names may work well here—for boys, David, after the energetic creative force David Byrne, and for girls, Tina, after the bassist admired by women and men alike.

The Songs

Angel	*Thank You for Sending Me an Angel*
Bill	*Bill*
Ruby	*Ruby Dear*

The Group

Chris	Chris Frantz
David	David Byrne
Jerry	Jerry Harrison
Tina	Tina Weymouth

James Taylor

The easy name for boys is James, after not just the singer but rock's most famous lullaby, *Sweet Baby James*.

For girls, there's the traditional *Oh Susannah*, or *Sarah Maria*, or—a slight stretch required here—*Carolina* (i.e., Caroline) *on My Mind*.

The Songs

Caroline	*Carolina on My Mind*
David	*Little David*
James	*Sweet Baby James*
Jim	*Captain Jim's Drunken Dream*
Johnnie	*Johnnie Comes Back*
Kelly	*Machine Gun Kelly*
Maria	*Sarah Maria*
Mona	*Mona*
Sarah	*Sarah Maria*
Susannah	*Oh, Susannah*

10,000 Maniacs/
Natalie Merchant

The Songs

Candy	*Candy Everybody Wants*
Jack	*Hey Jack Kerouac*
Jezebel	*Jezebel*
Katrina	*Katrina's Fair*
Noah	*Noah's Dove*
Rose	*My Sister Rose*

The Group

Dennis	Dennis Drew
Jerome	Jerome Augustyniak
Natalie	Natalie Merchant
Rob	Rob Buck

Three Dog Night

Be careful singing any of these oldies to your kid—the three lead singers featured in this group always sounded like they were one syllable away from rupturing a vocal chord.

Still, for a group that's mostly slipped into obscurity, there are some memorable tunes here, suitable for naming a child. *Joy to the World* offers names for a boy or girl, and *Eli's Coming* is perfect for a boy who's so irresistible that a warning needs to be issued whenever he's in town.

The Songs

April	*Pieces of April*
Eli	*Eli's Coming*
Jeremiah	*Joy to the World*
Joy	*Joy to the World*
Samantha	*Lady Samantha*

The Group

Chuck	Chuck Negron
Cory	Cory Wells
Danny	Danny Hutton
Floyd	Floyd Sneed
Jimmy	Jimmy Greenspoon
Joe	Joe Schermie
Mike	Mike Allsup

Toto

For naming a girl, the biggest hit from this group's catalog is probably *Rosanna* (written by David Paich about fellow band member Steve Porcaro's girlfriend, actress Rosanna Arquette).

For boys, your best bet is probably from the group member's names.

The Songs

Angel	*Angel Don't Cry*
Angela	*Angela*
Anna	*Anna*
Carmen	*Carmen*
Dave	*Dave's Gone Skiing*
George/	*St. George and the Dragon*
Georgy	*Georgy Porgy*

Toto (cont'd)

The Songs

Lea	*Lea*
Lorraine	*Lorraine*
Pamela	*Pamela*
Rosanna	*Rosanna*

The Group (various)

Bobby	Bobby Kimball
David	David Hungate
	David Paich
Jeffrey	Jeffrey Porcaro
Mike	Mike Porcaro
Simon	Simon Phillips
Steve	Steve Lukather
	Steve Porcaro

Traffic

(*see* Steve Winwood)

U2

For U2 fans looking for the opportunity to have an alternative baby name, the group's member roster offers interesting possibilities. How many children on your block are named Bono, for instance?

Well, okay, maybe there are a few Bonos, but how about Edge?

The Songs

Angel	*Angel of Harlem*
Elvis	*Elvis Presley and America*
Gloria	*Gloria*
Joshua	*Joshua Tree (album)*
Scarlet	*Scarlet*
Violet	*Ultra Violet (Light My Way)*

The Group

Adam	Adam Clayton
Bono	Bono
Edge	The Edge
Larry	Larry Mullen, Jr.

Van Halen/David Lee Roth

The Songs

Jimmy	*Top Jimmy*
Romeo	*Romeo Delight*
Rose	*Yankee Rose*

The Group

Alex	Alex Van Halen
David	David Lee Roth
Eddie	Eddie Van Halen
Michael	Michael Anthony
Sammy	Sammy Hagar

Velvet Underground

(*see also* John Cale, Lou Reed)

The Songs

Bill	*Ferryboat Bill*
Jane	*Sweet Jane*
Lisa	*Lisa Says*
Ray	*Sister Ray*
Stephanie	*Stephanie Says*
Venus	*Venus in Furs*

The Group

John	John Cale
Lou	Lou Reed
Maureen	Maureen Tucker
Nico	Nico
Sterling	Sterling Morrison

Wham!

(*see* George Michael)

Who

"Who are you?" you may ask your unnamed newborn, and it's unlikely the child will be so helpful and shout back, "I'm Happy Jack!"

No matter, there are plenty of name candidates for Who fans, whether the baby is doctor material, resembles an insect, or has shaky hands.

Name your boy Tommy, and he'll be in the center of an entire opera. This isn't easy to do, unless you want a name like Don Giovanni.

The Songs

Athena	*Athena*
Baba	*Baba O'Reilly*
Billy	*Little Billy*
Boris	*Boris, the Spider*
Henry	*I Can't Reach You (Spotted Henry)*
Jack	*Happy Jack*
Jimmy	*Dr. Jimmy*
Kevin	*Cousin Kevin*
Lily	*Pictures of Lily*
Mary-Anne	*Mary-Anne with the Shaky Hands*
Rael	*Rael*
	Rael 2
Sally	*Sally Simpson*
Tommy	*Tommy Can You Hear Me*
	Tommy's Holiday Camp

The Group

John	John Entwistle
Keith	Keith Moon
Kenney	Kenney Jones
Pete	Pete Townshend
Roger	Roger Daltrey

Steve Winwood

(includes Spencer Davis Group, Traffic, Blind Faith)

Winwood, the brilliant Brit who was in more sixties supergroups than anyone except for Eric Clapton, contributed his share of songs for baby names, especially for girls, and especially with the hit *Valerie*.

Steve Winwood (cont'd)

For boy names, there's always Steve and Stevie—not to mention the names of the members of all the groups he was in.

The Songs

Angel	*Help Me Angel*
Georgia	*Georgia on My Mind*
Grace	*State of Grace*
John	*John Barleycorn*
Pearl	*Pearly Queen*
Stevie	*Stevie's Blues*
Valerie	*Valerie*

The Groups

Spencer Davis Group

Muff	Muff Winwood
Peter	Peter York
Spencer	Spencer Davis
Steve	Steve Winwood

Traffic

Chris	Chris Wood
Dave	Dave Mason
Jim	Jim Capaldi
Steve	Steve Winwood

Blind Faith

Eric	Eric Clapton
Ginger	Ginger Baker
Rick	Rick Grech
Steve	Steve Winwood

Stevie Wonder

For girls, you can choose for your little *cherie amour* from several Wonder-ous tunes, many reflecting the singer's unflagging optimism—like *Joy* and *Pearl*.

For boys, it has to be Stevie—unless, for some reason, you want to want to name your son after the object of *You Haven't Done Nothin'*, and that would be President Nixon.

The Songs

Angel	*Angel Baby (Don't You Ever Leave)*
Angie	*Angie Girl*
Joy	*Joy (Takes Over Me)*
Maria	*Ave Maria*
Pearl	*Pearl*
Richard	*You Haven't Done Nothin'*
Sylvia	*Sylvia*

Neil Young

One of the most enduring rockers in the free world, Neil Young offers not only a few appropriate songs for naming your child, but the rich and varied styles he's mastered, from folk rock to grunge to country.

You could even name your child Johnny, *a la* Johnny One Note, for Neil's legendarily redundant guitar solos.

The Songs

Betty	*Betty Lou's Got a New Pair of Shoes*
Hank	*From Hank to Hendrix*
John	*Farmer John*
Lou	*Betty Lou's Got a New Pair of Shoes*
Pocahontas	*Pocahontas*

Zappa / Mothers

Frank Zappa already has some notoriety about baby names, having named two of his children Dweezil and Moon Unit. (He wasn't the first to get attention this way: see Jefferson Airplane/Starship.)

If Zappa is your inspiration for baby names, then let's face it, you have some fabulous candidates—for babies as big as mountains, babies who have good-sized limbs, or babies who are always kidding around.

Suzy is certainly hard to top, and "Creamcheese" would be all but required as a middle name.

The Songs

Andy	*Andy*
Bernie	*Uncle Bernie's Farm*
Billy	*Billy the Mountain*
Deseri	*Deseri*
Eddie	*Eddie Are Your Kidding?*
Emma	*Big Leg Emma*
Eric	*The Eric Dolphy Memorial Barbeque*
Evelyn	*Evelyn the Modified Dog*
Igor	*Igor's Boogie, Phase One and Two*
Jemima	*Electric Aunt Jemima*
Magdalena	*Magdalena*
Suzy	*Son of Suzy Creamcheese*
Valarie	*Valarie*

ZZ Top

There are numerous girl names for fans of this trio from Texas.

For boy names, you'll have to go to the group, especially if you have identical triple boys, each with a long beard. In this case, you're required to name them Billy, Dusty, and Frank.

The Songs

Esther	*Esther Be the One*
Francine	*Francine*
Kakkie	*Snappy Kakkie*
Leila	*Leila*
Pearl	*Apologies to Pearly*

The Group

Billy	Billy Gibbons
Dusty	Dusty Hill
Frank	Frank Beard

AND BABY MAKES THREE...
COMPREHENSIVE GUIDES BY
TRACIE HOTCHNER

PREGNANCY PURE&SIMPLE

77434-8/$11.00 US/$15.00 CAN

PREGNANCY & CHILDBIRTH

Revised Edition

78039-9/$12.50 US/$16.50 CAN

THE PREGNANCY DIARY

76543-8/$12.50 US/$16.50 CAN

The Groundbreaking #1
New York Times Bestseller by
ADELE FABER & ELAINE MAZLISH

"Have I got a book for you!...Run, don't walk, to your
nearest bookstore."
Ann Landers

SIBLINGS WITHOUT RIVALRY
How to Help Your Children Live Together So You Can Live Too
79900-6/$12.00 US/$16.00 Can

Don't miss their landmark book

HOW TO TALK SO KIDS WILL LISTEN AND LISTEN SO KIDS WILL TALK
57000-9/$12.50 US/$16.50 Can

"Will get more cooperation from children than all the yelling
and pleading in the world." *Christian Science Monitor*

and also

LIBERATED PARENTS, LIBERATED CHILDREN
71134-6/$11.00 US/$15.00 Can